C000090361

WHEN HORSES WERE SUPREME

The Age of the Working Horse

by
Herbert L. Day

HUTTON PRESS
1985

Hutton Press Ltd.
130 Canada Drive, Cherry Burton, Beverley
North Humberside, HU17 7SB

First Published 1985
Reprinted 1988, 1990, 1993

Printed by Clifford Ward & Co.
(Bridlington) Ltd.
55 West Street, Bridlington, East Yorkshire
YO15 3DZ

ISBN 0 907033 30 X

ILLUSTRATIONS

SUMMER CHANGES

In March better weather is on the way,
The Winter months have had their sway.
Soon it will be Spring,
Larks flying high will sing,
Horses pull sets of harrows
Which break up the furrow ridges.
When the seed drills appear,
Corn is sown for another year.
In April hedges are at their best,
Providing cover for birds' nests.
Grass grows longer every day,
Horses are stalled of dry corn and hay.
When the weather becomes warmer
They will feed on grass during the Summer.
May changes the country scene:
Corn fields become a luscious green.
Cows graze in the meadows
While men cultivate the dusty fallows.
When the sun is blazing down
Horses sweat but still work on.
When their working day comes to an end,
In grass fields the night they will spend.
In June the work is more steady,
Soon the fallows will be ready,
So clean without a weed
For a turnip drill to sow the seed.
When straight green lines come into view
The young shoots have broken through.
Before the month has passed
Hoeing the plants will be the task.
In July the corn produces ears
And the promise of harvest appears.
Before the ears have ripened,
Turnips have been hoed and scruffled.
There is still some time to spare
While the harvest is underway.
Men and horses can take a well-earned rest.
This time of the year was the best.

H. L. Day

5

CHAPTER ONE

I recall with nostalgia my boyhood days spent on my Uncle Bill's farm before 1914, when life was slow and meaningful and the natural beauty of the countryside remained unspoilt. There were leafy lane approaches to villages and narrow winding roads. There were fields — each one surrounded by hawthorn hedges — which created a crazy paving pattern across the countryside. Birds found cover for their nests, and small animals — weasels, rabbits, and the like — found hiding places in the hedge-bottoms. Wild flowers haunted by insects were a common sight.

The roads were friendly places. Friends and relations walking towards a village in order to attend a place of worship occupied the full width of the road. Flocks of sheep and other stock were driven to market with little inconvenience. Road vehicles travelled at the speed of horses, and farmers relied on them when cultivating the land. It was not unusual to see two farmers in conversation while sitting in their respective traps, wheel to wheel, with their horses' heads pointing in opposite directions.

A market was held in every town, and it was a weekly event in the lives of the farming community. Monday was Market Day at Pickering, our local town, and in the morning fat and store cattle were sold. In the afternoon business concerned with farming took place. Market Day was referred to as "Cobbler's Monday," because many made it an excuse to have a break from their weekly routine. It was attended by local village tradesmen and also by casual workers hoping to catch the eye of a farmer who required extra hands.

Horses and traps conveying farmers, their wives, and most likely a basket of butter and eggs, entered the town from all directions. There were no fixed prices for produce and most of the farmers' business was conducted in the Market Place. They sold their cereals to a merchant who supplied them with feeding stuffs and other requirements. A barter system was practised, and money only changed hands to balance the difference.

A farmer would carry a sample of grain in a small cloth bag and displayed a handful to a merchant. He would examine it for quality and fixed the price accordingly. A farmer had no alternative but to accept the price offered. Best quality wheat made 36/- a quarter, with 18 stones in each sack; oats fetched 21/- a quarter, with 12 stones in each sack, and barley 35/- a quarter, with 16 stones in each sack.

A barter system was also practised between a farmer's wife and the shopkeeper to whom she sold her produce and from whom she obtained her provisions. At the rear of the Black Swan was a yard with stables where a horse and trap could be "put up" for a shilling a day. An ostler in attendance arranged the position of the traps, stabled the horses, and collected the fees.

Occasionally a farmer would arrive at the yard incapable, after having had one too many in the course of completing his day's business. The ostler then yoked his horse for him and let it out of the yard. He set it off in the right direction and relied on the horse to take its master safely home. Such incidents were not uncommon, yet I can only recall one occasion when there was a mishap.

Due to his drinking habits, Jim Atkin's farm was in a neglected state. He owned a trap mare called Polly, and a more faithful animal never existed. She was often seen on a night — yoked to the trap — standing outside the Black Bull. In the Winter Jim covered her with sacks, but in any case Polly would never have left him. She had always taken him safely home, even when he was too drunk to hold the reins, except on one occasion which turned out to be the last.

For some unknown reason Polly's near-side rein became taut and steered her to the side of the road. The wheel of the trap mounted a bank and the trap turned over. Fortunately the shafts broke off and Polly escaped injury, but Jim was trapped underneath. When my Uncle Bill arrived on the scene, Polly, with the broken shafts attached to her harness, was looking down mournfully at Jim, who was shouting his head off. After his release he staggered home, with the mare following him like a dog.

It was no surprise to local farmers when Jim's creditors foreclosed on him and sold his live and dead stock. Uncle Bill, who attended the sale, informed me that Jim cried when Polly came under the auctioneer's hammer.

Kirby Misperton village and the surrounding farms known as the Kirby Misperton estate were owned by Mr Twentyman. He was the one in authority, but if a farmer respected the lease of his tenancy he was the master on his farm. When Mr Twentyman travelled further afield, he rode in a gig to Pickering station in order to board a train. The horse, a high-stepping hackney, was driven by his coachman. The vehicle, harness and horse were all in immaculate condition. The two passengers rode side by side "stiff-backed" and looked straight ahead and never spoke. John Richmond described them thus: "They look like a couple of statues." On his return journey the coachman was relaxed and acknowledged friends and acquaintances as he passed them by.

The village stores supplied the majority of the villagers' requirements, otherwise it meant a journey to Pickering. No-one to my knowledge owned a bike, and there was no bus service or convenient railway. "Shank's pony" was the only way to travel.

Tailor Ward made to measure everyone's clothes and also supplied the farming community. When attending the funeral of a deceased, relatives always wore black. Tailor Ward often worked late into the night to complete an order. Hired lads from a nearby farm visited his shop, and no doubt he was glad to have their company. The farm lads rarely wore cloth in the Winter, preferring corduroy. They wore bell-bottom trousers, which were tight at the knees. The width at the bottom varied between 21 and 30 inches. Some were made of velvet, and stitched to the outside seam near the bottom of each leg were three pearl buttons.

At the Pickering Hirings, wagoners, after a few pints under their belts, swaggered down the Market Place as if they owned the town, with their trousers flapping over their boot tops.

The village joiner Mr Mortimer, nicknamed "Mutt," made shafts and handles for the tools required on a farm. He also made swingle-trees, cobble-trees, wagons and carts. He relied on the blacksmiths to make the iron fittings, and they worked in conjunction when hooping wheels.

The village was a peaceful place. Occasionally there was the jingle of harness, the clip-clop of horses' feet and the sound of wagon wheels. You could even lie down and go to sleep in the middle of the road. This may result in a rough awakening by the driver of a horse-drawn vehicle, but there was no risk of injury. The sound most frequently heard throughout the day was the ring of the blacksmith's hammer as it came into contact with iron and the anvil. There was no illumination in the street and, during the Winter, social events — most of which were centred around the chapel — were arranged to coincide with a full moon.

There was a farming community spirit in the true sense of the word, and tenants rallied round a neighbour experiencing a difficult period. The majority of mares foaled when Spring sowing was in full swing. A mare was always a risk and the loss of one was felt most keenly on a small farm where there would probably be straitened circumstances. If a mare became a casualty and the owner could not find a replacement, a neighbour with a horse to spare would loan it to him free of charge. This arrangement was referred to as "meat for work."

A new tenant was given a ploughing day which took place in March. Every farmer on the estate sent his teams and men. Similar help was given to a farmer at harvest who had stooks in his fields after his neighbours had gathered all in.

Shire horses were in their hey-day. The breeding had reached a high standard, and the population was at its peak. There was continual demand for dray horses required by town firms, and farmers were encouraged to breed them. At the census taken in 1910 in England there were 834,064 horses and brood mares used solely for agricultural purposes, 224,284 unbroken young horses, and 93,974 foals, making a total of 1,152,322.

CHAPTER TWO

The landed gentry played a major part in the breeding of pure-bred Shire horses. On many of their estates there was a Home Farm, which functioned as a stud and only pedigree stock was kept. The best colt foals were retained as stallions, and once they were three years old they were ready for service. Each year from April 1st until the end of June the service of a stallion was available to every farmer in the country. On Lord Middleton's estate near Malton there was a stud farm, and every season his stallions were travelled in the Malton-York area and on the adjacent Wolds.

Recognised horse dealers retained by town firms visited the farms in a certain area which corresponded to their source of supply.

The photograph on the following page is one to turn a man's thoughts down memory lane if he had worked as a farm horseman in the pre-tractor era.

A layman might look on the photo as being similar to many of its kind featuring a ploughing scene, but a horseman would recognise it as being something different.

At a glance he would know that the horse in the foreground was a somewhat raw three-year-old — its ungainly stance and its head held as high as possible are clues. No doubt these and the horse's bewildered look were the result of strange objects suddenly catching its eye — probably the tri-pod camera and the hood which covered the photographer's head!

It would also be obvious, by the unusual manner in which the two horses had been coupled together, that the young one was in a stage of being schooled. Instead of its halter being attached to the ring on its opposite number's hame, it had been tied to the trace.

When this procedure was practised and the plough-string attached, its bit was held firmly and the horse could be restrained from forging ahead, otherwise its energy was sapped unnecessarily. It was essential to train a young one to continually pull the plough at a regular pace.

The old horse standing in the furrow in the photo has little in common with its young partner and its placidness is evident. This and the horse's exceptional intelligence would be the reasons why it had been selected as a partner for unschooled horses.

In the earliest stages, turning a young horse anti-clockwise was often a problem, for when pressure was put on its bit it often turned its head only. I came across many an old horse which used to push a young one round. If this had not been so, iron shoes and horses' legs would have come into contact and injuries could have resulted.

Once a horse had been trained to work in traces it became a valuable property. From being a foal its fodder had been an expense, but later it would earn its keep and its value would increase.

A ploughing scene, 1910, on a farm near Walkington, Beverley.

During this period, when required, it would be yoked to a pole wagon and when the horse had become accustomed to working between a pair of shafts its schooling would be complete.

The photo on the preceding page was taken during a period when there was a demand for dray horses. A good price could be obtained for a five-year-old which could be guaranteed as being "sound in wind and limb" and "quiet in all gears."

It was the hired workers' knowledge, ability, patience and their devotion to the animals which brought the horses' schooling to a satisfactory conclusion.

Village tradesmen, corn merchants, dealers and many more business people relied on the farming community for their prosperity, but none were more conspicuous in their appearance than the horse dealers. When going about their legitimate business they were always dressed in breeches, black leggings and boots. A dealer was never seen without a hard hat and a walking stick.

The first week in January was the ideal period for a farmer to sell his horses. This would enable the three-year-olds which replaced them to be schooled to work before the Spring sowing. A dealer who supplied reputable town firms with dray horses would only consider those in peak condition. When he arrived at a farm the wagoner was detailed to parade the horse for sale. If it was the type the dealer required he examined it soundly, and a good action was essential.

I remember one, George Humble by name, whose knowledge of horses was second to none. His services as a judge were in great demand when agricultural shows were being held. Wagoners referred to George as "awd honey," not because they had any regard for him — far from it. He used these words when he spoke to them, but as far as they were concerned he was the one who robbed them of their best horses. It took two years to school a young one and when the full training was completed it was fully developed and was five years old. At this age a horse was at its best and a joy to drive. Its awkwardness and the extra work involved in the early stages was forgotten.

When George was in the vicinity of a railway goods yard and noticed it was full of farm wagons, he would wander round the horses. If he saw one of the type he required he would approach the wagoner concerned and say: "That's a nice horse you've got, honey." Then he would try to obtain such information as the horse's age, whether it was sound and docile and had been yoked between a pair of shafts attached to a cart. On the occasions when he questioned me I remained silent.

Some of the wagoners I knew cribbed the horse, and it was not unusual for George to be told where to go in no uncertain manner. This did not upset him and he always had the last word: "Don't get excited, honey."

Before he departed he wrote down the name and address painted on the wagon. It was only a matter of time before he appeared at the farm and a wagoner could say goodbye to one of his pair of horses.

The last time I saw George was in 1947. I was driving a horse yoked to a cart along Hungate, Pickering. He was standing on the footpath, an old man of ninety, dressed in his traditional clothes. He gazed with admiration at the horse, and I expected him to say: "That's a nice horse you've got, honey."

He represented a bygone age when horses were supreme. Fortunately he was not destined to live and witness the wholesale slaughter of horses which was soon to follow.

Horses being examined by a horse-dealer. Also in picture is the farmer and his wagoner.

14

The railways had the monopoly of long-distance freight, which included animals. The railway which linked the two market towns of Malton and Driffield provided a service for Wold farmers, whose land covered a wide area. The small, reliable engines hauled the wagons and carriages up and down the hills. When the train left Burdale station for Malton it passed through a tunnel and the carriages were illuminated.

Every morning a goods train left each town, hauling wagons containing farmers' requirements such as coal, feeding stuffs, or fertilisers. Wagons were left at the scheduled intermediate stations. In the afternoon, on the train's return journey, wagons for dispatch were collected, loaded with farmers' sold produce. The goods yards were a hive of industry, especially in the Winter, when corn was threshed. Cattle kept in buildings required more feeding stuff than when they were outdoors in the Summer. Coal was a farmer's only source of energy, and on a threshing day he had to supply the fuel required to steam the engine.

Goods were conveyed to and from the stations on farm wagons, each one drawn by four horses. On Market Days the passenger trains were well patronised by the farming community. Baskets containing butter and eggs, and perhaps a crate of chickens, were carried in the guard's van; he often had a calf for company too. It was placed in a bag, the mouth of which was tied loosely round its neck. Although its movements were restricted, it was able to lie comfortably and contentedly.

During Martinmas Week, single workers travelled on the trains in order to attend a Hirings Day at Malton or Driffield. The last train to leave on one of these occasions was always full. Hired workers who were a bit merry were pushed into the carriages by the guard and porters. When the train arrived at a station, the farewells between friends as they parted echoed around. "Tack care a thi sen an arl see tha ageean some tarm," they shouted to each other as the train moved off into the darkness.

The 1914 harvest in this part of Yorkshire was one of the most difficult experienced in living memory. It was unique in this respect: farmers lost key workers practically in a matter of minutes. They were members of Sir Mark Sykes of Sledmere's "Wagoners Reserve," a horse transport unit he formed in 1912. He recruited the majority of the members from the big farms in the area on each side of the railway. The unit was commandeered by the army soon after war was declared on August 4th, 1914.

Harvest was early that year and cutting was in full swing. When the food baskets arrived in the field they contained the wagoners' calling-up papers. Those affected immediately left their horses yoked to binders in order to report to army depots, where they received their kit.

The wagoners did not receive any special army training, and their unit

Two horses ploughing, later commandeered by the Army in 1915.

was among the first to be sent to France. When they had attended the Hirings, the wagoners could never have dreamt that one day they would be sent overseas to fight for their country, departing from all the intermediate stations on the Wold railway.

The army required a continuous supply of horses, and many of those sent to France suffered cruelty and death, which could not be avoided. Those which were commandeered in this area were despatched from these same Wold stations.

The source of supply for these horses were the farms, and farmers had no option but to sell. They were paid fifty guineas per horse, later increased to fifty-five. Recognised horse buyers were appointed, and each one was allocated the farms in a certain area. The horses they bought were kept in remount depots until the army sent for them.

The depots were situated at the rear of public houses, where there were large stables which had previously accommodated farmers' horses and traps on Market Days. This turned out to be an unsatisfactory arrangement because of the long waiting periods involved. There was the expense of fodder and the keepers' wages, and the horses also became soft through lack of work.

If they were not exercised, a Shire's hind legs were inclined to swell, and some of them developed an irritating complaint known as "grease." Washing their legs with sheep dip was the only treatment I knew for this. Otherwise a horse would rub its legs together until the skin broke. If one horse began to cough, soon all the rest in the stable were coughing too.

Mr Robinson, one of the buyers, realised that it would be better to leave the horses on the farm where they had been bought until they were required. If a farmer was allowed to keep and work them, the horses would retain their working condition at no expense to the army.

A conference was held at York, and Mr Robinson was invited to attend. The army authorities heard and accepted his suggestions, and the depots were closed down. A farmer received a telegram when horses were required, and they were put on rail at the nearest station. The man responsible for putting them on the train received five shillings for each horse he despatched.

In peace time, horses were conveyed in specially designed box wagons. Inside were three partitions, which enabled each horse to stand in a stall. At one end of the wagon was a small compartment which provided accommodation for a groom, who had a good view of the horses. Due to the increased war traffic, there were not enough box wagons, and many horses were transported in cattle trucks. They stood across these head to tail alternately, and were made secure with halters.

When the wagoner on the farm where I was hired in 1916 despatched horses in cattle trucks he removed their halters. This comparative freedom allowed the horses a more comfortable journey. The top of the cattle truck was covered with a taurpaulin sheet, and there was a narrow opening which enabled the horses to obtain a glimpse of the passing countryside. But this was to be their last look: they were travelling to France, journey's end.

In peace time a farmer would not allow a horse to be worked until it was rising three years old, otherwise its growth was retarded. This could not be taken into consideration in war time. Empty stalls had to be filled regardless, and two-year-old horses were brought into the stables as replacements. There was no joy in driving young horses of this age. Although they were yoked to the lightest implements, their tiredness was evident before the end of the day.

When I see in print such village names as Wetwang or Fimber I am reminded of the bygone railway and its intermediate stations. I am also reminded of the farm horses which were taken to France never to return, and of the courage and sacrifice of the Wagoners Reserves. Their contribution to the war effort should never be forgotten.

Horses being despatched to war in converted cattle trucks.

19

CHAPTER FOUR

One fine Summer's day in 1970, I stood on a road about a mile from the Wold village of Thixendale, and gazed across a valley. Eventually I recognised Broadholme Farm where I was the hired wagoner in the mid 1920s. I could also see the road on which I had driven four horses yoked to a wagon when travelling to or from Burdale station.

Thixendale lies in a hollow, and is surrounded by hillside. In the depth of Winter, daylight fades early in the afternoons. No lamps were carried on the wagon, and there were occasions when the horses pulled it the last mile uphill from the village to the farm in total darkness. If there was any legislation regarding the carrying of lamps on wagons or haycarts, it was not enforced to my knowledge.

After a heavy fall of snow the village was one of the first in the area to be isolated. The road between Thixendale and Burdale station was always a difficult passage for horses in these conditions. One afternoon when I was on my way to collect a load of cattle cake, the snow was thawing. While I was loading my wagon in the goods yard, it began to freeze and my return journey was a nightmare.

There was no alternative. In order to control my team I had to ride my nearside pole horse and drive the leading pair from this position. I rode without my feet in the stirrups, ready to jump clear should the horse lose its footing. Occasionally its hind feet slipped forward under its belly, but the horse carried me safely to Thixendale.

I dare not attempt the hill which was the last lap of my journey, so I stopped at the blacksmith's shop. He removed two nails from each of the horses' shoes and replaced them with stud nails, 32 in all. It was dark, so he worked with the aid of a stable lamp. The horses were now able to pull the wagon with more confidence, and I was relieved of my anxiety. Nevertheless they were lathered with sweat before I arrived at the farm, and no doubt fear had played its part.

Broadholme was a good place for hired workers, and for the horses too. There were no restrictions regarding fodder, and the six in my stable were in peak condition. All the grain sold was put on rail at Burdale station, and on one particular day I was transporting 15 quarters of barley — 30 sacks. Wet weather had held up ploughing, so the horses had had a rest period and were in high spirits.

In order to enter the goods yard, I had to pass under the railway through an archway, then turn left up a short incline. After I had emptied my load, I attached the lock chain to the nearside wheel. This caused it to sledge down the incline and act as a brake. When I had passed through the archwway I stopped and removed the chain. As I was mounting my saddle horse, a motor-bike and side-car appeared through the tunnel and the driver blew his horn. The startled horses broke into a gallop before I had a chance to grab the reins.

I shudder to think what the consequence would have been if I had failed to mount the horse. Eventually, when the horses felt the pressure on their bits, they steadied down to their natural gait, but I did not allow the motor-cyclist to pass until I arrived at Thixendale, when I gave him a piece of my mind.

Wagons have become obsolete on the Wold farms, and there are very few remaining landmarks of the Driffield-Malton railway. Today Burdale station is unrecognisable as such: the site is covered with wild growth and the buildings are in ruins. It is difficult to imagine that there was once a goods yard there which was a hive of activity.

CHAPTER FIVE

In January 1915, three seventeen-year-old village lads left the farms where they were hired. They joined the army, and were eventually sent to France. It so happened that Tom was the only one who could read and write. The mothers of Ted and Dick had to rely on his letters for news of their sons. They were notified by the postman when he had one to deliver, and the three mothers soon joined each other.

Ted was courting Mary, the servant girl employed at the Home Farm, and he had to rely on Tom to write his love letters. "Jist wreet love an sike" had been Ted's instructions.

When peace was declared in 1918, Tom returned home alone; his pals had been buried in Flanders. Ted stopped a sniper's bullet, but Dick's death was to some extent a mystery. Always the lad for a bit of poaching, he had raided French farmers' hen runs after dark. One night he failed to return, and he was found shot in the vicinity of a farm.

No doubt the letters Tom had written to Mary had found favour in her eyes, because within a month of his return they were married. He became the foreman at Home Farm, and she continued her employment as the servant. Mary was a thrifty soul, and she persuaded Tom to bank the gratuity he received after being demobbed. They both continued to save until eventually they had sufficient capital to enable them to obtain the lease of Manor Farm.

Bill Boyde was recognised as being one of the best wagoners in the Holderness area, and he enlisted in 1915. He served throughout the war, and after peace was declared he became the foreman at Bush Farm.

In the Summer the horses were collected in the pasture, brought into the stable and prepared for work before breakfast was served. One particular morning a four-year-old horse was standing in the pasture unable to move. When Bill approached it, he realised that the horse's nearside front hoof had practically been torn off. He searched the field and eventually found the horse's hoof and shoe wedged in a rabbit hole. While attempting to release itself the horse had panicked and its injury was the result.

Bill was ordered to have the injured animal put down, but instead he decided to give it attention in his leisure time. He prepared a warm bran mash in a small bag, and placed the injured foot in it, then secured the bag round the horse's leg. Every day Bill fed and watered the horse in the pasture, and when necessary exchanged the bran for a fresh supply.

The boss had noticed these activities, and one day he remarked: "I see we still have that injured horse." After Bill had informed him that it was doing well and should be allowed to grow a new hoof, he agreed, but only on condition that no outside expenses should be incurred such as a vet's fee.

A year later, Bill — with extreme satisfaction — was able to send for a

Bill Boyde ploughing in 1911.

23

blacksmith, who trimmed the new hoof and fixed a shoe to it. Once again the horse could be guaranteed sound. It was sold to a dealer who supplied town firms with dray horses, but there was no reward for Bill, only self-satisfaction.

In July 1915 I left school, and when the hay was ready to cock, I gathered it into rows with a horse-rake. I drove the horses as I walked behind, and when I jacked up the rake I had to stride over the hay it had gathered. The following Summer Bill replaced the rake with a new one, which had a seat fixed to it. I was able to ride and sing or whistle as I drove Daisy — yoked to the rake — across a field.

1916 was the first year that British Summer Time came into force. Our hens had free range during the day and returned to their huts to roost when the evening shadows began to fall. The new time did not affect their habits, and they stayed out an hour longer. Then they were at risk from a prowling fox which, given half a chance, would pick a hen up. Fortunately, our dog Punch could round up the hens in the same way as sheep, and they soon disappeared into their huts when the dog began to perform.

The new time was not popular with the majority of farmers, especially at hay-time or harvest. Leading either produce home could not begin until the dew had dried off. This, of course, was an hour later when the clock time was an hour ahead of the sun. One farmer I knew would not allow BST to be practised, and his men did not relish working an hour after those employed on neighbouring farms had returned home. When his hired hands received their pay on Martinmas Day, some would not return for a second year. Word was passed round at the Hirings, and he had to promise the men he engaged that he would practise BST.

This was the year conscription came into force, and the armed forces drained the farms of single men aged eighteen years or over, as very few failed their medicals. Townsmen who were rejected were directed to work on the land, and the majority were more bother than they were worth. Their knowledge of horses was practically nil, and they had no idea how to harness, yoke or drive them. Farmers certainly had their labour problems, and at the Hirings experienced lads under military age were in great demand.

In 1916 the war was at its height, and casualties were heavy on land and sea. The horses commandeered and sent to France were being slaughtered wholesale to such an extent that British farmers were unable to meet the army's demands. Canadian horses were imported, and for the original owners this was a good chance to get rid of their "wrong-uns" — those that were vicious and liable to kick or savage a man without warning. The blacksmith who shod my uncle's horses practised at Pickering, and when he was shoeing one of these imported horses he suffered a serious injury.

Our mare Daisy had brittle hooves, and one day she threw a shoe. I was detailed to lead her to Pickering on the grass verge wherever possible, in order to protect the shoeless hoof. My destination was a strange blacksmith's shop. When I arrived, the smith asked me my name and also my uncle's name and address. The price for shoeing a horse all round with new shoes was 10/-, fixing an odd one was 2/6 — a half-crown coin.

Bill had given me the required coin, and as soon as I had handed it over, the smith dropped it on the anvil, and it turned out to be a dud. He told me that he had accepted a similar coin the previous week, and each one he had received since then he had dropped on the anvil.

The following Market Day, Bill paid his debt, and the blacksmith agreed to accept any further work Bill required doing. In the future he paid his bills quarterly, but when I visited the shop with a horse the smith never failed to ask: "Have you brought me another dud half-crown?"

At the Martinmas Hirings held at Pickering in 1916, a farmer engaged me to be his wagoner's lad and I never visited the blacksmith's shop in Park Street again.

Hired horsemen, from left to right: Wagoner, his lad, Thoddy, his lad.

CHAPTER SIX

Farmers hired single hands to work from the first week in December until Martinmas Day, November 23rd, when they received their yearly wage. Included was the payment for the extra hours worked at harvest and in the stables. Horses were prepared for work before the recognised day's work began, and in the evening they received after-care and attention.

This method benefited farmers: the hired workers were provided with their board, they lived in the respective farmhouses and were therefore at hand to attend to the horses. In order to keep an eye on a sick horse or a mare due to foal during the night, I used to cat-nap in the kitchen, and the next day it was work as usual.

It was possible to manage a farm comprising 500 acres with eighteen working horses, but it was essential to keep them in good condition. Otherwise they would not have developed the stamina necessary to do the work required of them.

A farmer had no problems in this respect if he allowed his feeders sufficient fodder. The horses were divided into units of six; a man and a lad could expect this to be the number in their stable. Each horseman had his own recognised pair of plough horses, an arrangement which benefited the farmer concerned, because the horses received the best care and attention.

An understanding relationship developed between a man and his horses which cannot be experienced with a machine. If a pair of horses were of different temperaments, they would work together in harmony if handled in the correct manner.

Due to his seniority, the wagoner had the pick of the horses and, of course, he selected the most outstanding pair. He ensured that they were always in peak condition, and he would not allow anyone else to handle them.

When a team was yoked to a wagon, his horses were the leading pair. Unlike the two pole horses they were not subjected to the strain experienced when steadying a loaded wagon downhill .A wagoner would not consider yoking either of his horses between the shafts of a heavy cart. He ensured that no one else handled them except at harvest, when his lad drove them yoked to a binder.

It was essential to complete the sowing of Spring corn in the least possible time in order to "beat the weather." Otherwise there would be delays at harvest time. Cutting would be held up, and there would be a waiting period between crops until the corn was ripe.

Drilling the corn was the wagoner's responsibility, and this was one occasion when he was unable to nurse his horses. He had orders to push them to their limit. He was also responsible for selecting the horses for the work in hand. He had to take into consideration the type of implement in use and the state of the land, knowledge which could only be gained by experience.

Unlike machines, horses are flesh and blood, and are subject to nerves, physical disorders and pain. I found it impossible not to be concerned with the welfare of the horses which formed my working unit. I did not consider the work I did in the stable to be real work as such, and it was no place for a man who had no compassion or patience.

A certain amount of discipline was maintained, and a lad was not allowed to visit another stable when work was in progress. If he had done so, he would have been ordered in no uncertain terms to return.

On the Wolds, a road leading to a farm was repaired with chalk stones, and the surface became soft when it rained. When four horses yoked to a wagon travelled towards a farm, the splashes of chalk dried their legs and bodies white. Grooming horses in this state was the hardest work encountered in a stable, and a wagoner ensured that the job was done thoroughly.

I recall how proud I was when I received my first yearly wage on Martinmas Day in 1917. There were no stoppages, for my aunt had supplied me with pocket money, and I was therefore paid the full amount, £16. It was wartime, and farmers were receiving inflated prices for their produce and stock. Wages rose accordingly, and a wagoner who was able to evade conscription could obtain a yearly wage of £100.

Some lads were not so fortunate as myself, and they had to sub their pocket money. Nine times out of ten they only received half the amount they asked for. The year following my eighteenth birthday seven pence per week was stopped from my wages to cover my National Insurance stamp.

When I was a schoolboy I remember my grandfather quoting the saying: "Early to bed and early to rise makes a man healthy, wealthy and wise." All his life he practised this philosophy, and it was obvious that he had acquired wisdom, but wealth had eluded him. His greatest asset was his good health, and he claimed that he had never lost a day's work through illness. He lived to be eighty-five and only required medical attention during the last year of his life. He described the medicine he received thus: "It's nowt but coloured watta an a few Hepsam salts among it."

One night during the Summer of 1917 toothache kept me awake. Cultivating for turnips was in full swing, and the next day I was still in pain. The nearest dentist lived in a market town ten miles away. There was no convenient railway, and bus services were non-existent. If I had asked for time off, the foreman would have treated it as a joke. There was no alternative, I had to hike to the local doctor's surgery after supper. Incidentally, this was the only occasion that I required a doctor's attention during my hiring days.

It was a two-pronged tooth, and the doctor's wife assisted her husband in extracting it by holding my head firmly between her hands. I did not receive any pain-killing treatment, and was charged a shilling.

Every year, farm horsemen walked hundreds of miles as they followed the implements. No doubt this contributed to the good health that workers enjoyed in the horse-farming days.

Least lad, the youngest horseman, at work ploughing a rough, fallow field.

CHAPTER SEVEN

It was a hard life for a lad the first year he was hired to work and live on a farm, especially if his knowledge of horses was limited. He was allocated an old pair of horses and, to coin a phrase, "they had more off than he had."

I had no problem with horses reluctant to be geared with a collar, for I followed these instructions passed on to me by my grandfather — who was steeped in horse lore — before I left school: "Before a horse can raise its head high, slip the collar over one eye and cover the other. To regain its full sight the horse will thrust its head forward and the collar immediately slips over its ears." The collar was put on upside down, and turning it round the horse's neck was not difficult.

In later years, when I was in charge of a stable, a few threatening words from me would persuade a horse to lower its head, otherwise it could expect a few slaps on its rump.

A lad soon acquired patience, and a firm hand was essential to control a team. I never raised my voice to a horse unless I was displeased, then it understood and toed the line. When I was the "least lad" — the youngest — employed on Elm Tree Farm, John Harwick had this to say: "If I hadn't seen your horses moving in the field, I wouldn't have known you were there." I never pulled a rein or a plough string with force unless it was necessary. Having "good hands" with horses was a gift, and not all lads were blessed in this respect.

Turnips were produced to provide fodder for the cattle and sheep during the Winter, and every day a supply was carted from field to farm regardless of the prevailing weather. A lad was ordered to yoke two horses tandem fashion into a cart. When there was ice on the road, he had his share of anxiety wondering if one of his horses would lose its feet.

The trace horse was not hindered, but if the second horse slipped down it was trapped between the shafts. It was essential to restrain its attempts to get up, otherwise a back injury might result. The horse would lie still if its head was pressed firmly to the ground by kneeling on it. After the harness had been removed from the horse's collar and the breeching from the saddle, the remaining harness was not attached to the shafts. When the cart had been pushed backwards, with the shafts trailing on the ground, the horse was free, and if uninjured was soon on its feet again.

Help was required to free the horse, but this was soon on hand. It was natural for shepherds working in adjacent fields to follow the progress of a lad and his team, especially when the road was treacherous. An old horse which had learnt to take short strides and dig the toes of its front shoes into ice was usually yoked between the shafts, and consequently such an incident rarely occurred.

Candles and paraffin lamps were the only means of illumination, and yet

I never saw a farm on fire or heard of one. If a fire had taken place, especially in the Winter when all stock except sheep were kept in buildings, the result could have been disastrous. Stacks of corn, straw and hay would have been at risk, also animals would have been trapped in the buildings. Horses and cows tied up in stalls would have had little chance of escape.

The foreman and each horseman in charge of a stable were each issued with a lamp, and also the bullocky and the shepherd at lambing time. In a stable where there were stalls for six horses, one lamp provided poor illumination. It was suspended from a wire which was fixed to each end wall, and the lamp could be moved to the position required. Usually it was hung above the wagoner's pair, and I recall grooming my horses in semi-darkness.

It was essential to remove sweatmarks, especially those which had accumulated on a horse's shoulders, otherwise continual neglect might result in a sore. To ensure that this did not happen, my free hand practically followed the dandy-brush. I wore a corduroy suit and I worked in my waistcoat and the attached calico sleeves protected my shirt.

Stable lamps were used to illuminate the hired workers' bedroom, and I would often have to slink upstairs in the dark because I was too tired to wait until the wagoner was ready for bed. If I had not jumped out of bed quickly in the early hours of the following morning, and dressed in the least possible time, I should have been left in the dark. There were odd occasions when I was unable to lace my boots until we arrived at the stable. This happened before I realised that putting my clothes on while standing was the quickest way.

When an implement was being drawn across a field, the width of the land affected was known as a "breed." An established foreman knew how many "drill breeds" were required in each field in order to sow an acre. I was told at an early age: "Drive your horses as straight as possible across a field. Time is saved, and horses benefit too." It was the ambition of all horse lads to plough a straight furrow and create straight lines regardless of the type of implement in use.

Strict time-keeping was practised, and if horsemen left the stable late or returned home at noon or night with time in hand, there would be complaints from the foreman. There were no such things as alarm clocks on farms, and I used to rise on time regularly through force of habit. In the Spring and Summer, a pocket watch was necessary because work on the land was taking place in different fields. In Winter such a situation did not arise when ploughing was in progress. The teams were not separated, and the wagoner was the time-keeper.

When Spring corn was a few inches high it was rolled in order to secure the roots firmly into the ground and to preserve moisture. The implement used was called a "flat roller." Four sections were fixed to a frame, and attached to this was a pole. Rolling corn was recognised as a "least lad's" job, and when a field was completed it was an attractive sight.

The alternate "breeds" laid the corn alternate ways too, and two different shades of green were created. The breeds were straight too. Alas, corn does not get such treatment today, and such a scene will never be witnessed again.

A lad on his "fost year off" could not afford a watch, and he had to rely on men working in an adjacent field to give him a shout when it was time to "loose out." Before 1920, the watches owned by countrymen were known as "English levers," a solid, heavy and reliable watch referred to as a "tunnup" by hired workers.

I never knew the initial cost, but in 1924 I bought an English lever second-hand for £3. No doubt it was a prestige watch because the face was embossed to resemble flowers and the hands made of gold. Inside the watch had been inscribed these words: "J. Hill. Kirkbymoorside. Made 1871."

When a village tailor made a pair of trousers, he attached cross pockets, and above the right-hand-side one a smaller pocket. A watch was carried in this, and the chain attached to it dangled down into the pocket below. When a lad was asked: "Wot tarm is it by thy awd tonnup?" he would produce his watch with a flourish which caused the medallion at the end of the chain to swing like a pendulum.

In the 1920s, Ingersol watches, which did not require a key to wind the Spring, flooded the shops. The price of 5/- for a watch was good value for money. I was fortunate in that before I left home for my first place, my Uncle Bill presented me with his watch.

When Martinmas Day arrived, a least lad received his first year's wage. When he attended the Hirings held in the local town, he was able to buy clothes and boots to act as replacements for the coming year. Perhaps among his purchases would be a pair of horse-brasses, a pocket-knife, and certainly a watch.

If he had agreed to "to stop again" he would say "no" to a farmer who accosted him and asked: "Dis thoo want hiring lad?" He could enjoy the fun of the fair in a carefree manner — the swings and steam roundabouts which had been erected in the town.

CHAPTER EIGHT

The countryside is losing its old-time characters, and their quaint sayings are dying out too. For example, there used to be a saying: "Light Michaelmas, Dark Martinmas, Light Christmas." When it was vice versa and there was a full moon during Martinmas, there were frosts at night and crisp, fine days; otherwise there was damp weather and dull days.

On December 3rd 1918 I rode my bike to Abbey Farm and had to contend with ice-bound roads. If my bike had slipped from under me there was practically no risk of being run over, for in those days a motor was a rare sight.

I arrived at the farm soon after 3.00 p.m. and found Jim Rogers (thoddy) and his lad, Alf Johnson, had beaten me to it. Soon after, Fred Keast (wagoner) turned up and we adjourned to the saddle-room. I was well acquainted with Fred — we had lived on adjacent farms — but the other two were strangers.

Names and addresses were exchanged, and we were soon on friendly terms. This was to be my third year off, and I learnt that it would be Alf's second. We discussed the farms we had left, and those we had lived and worked on in previous years, but the main part of our conversation concerned horses.

At 4.00 p.m. we made our way to our respective stables, and six horses were kept in each of them. They were as fat as pigs, and, as for size, I had never had to deal with horses so big. Neither Alf nor myself could have imagined the trials and tribulations which were in store for us. We sat on the corn bin waiting for the foreman to arrive and pass on to us information such as each horse's name and age.

The original Abbey, situated in a paddock, had been converted into a dwelling house, and was occupied by the foreman and his family. This was the place where we ate and slept. Most of our leisure time was spent in the saddle-room.

One July day in 1969 I returned to Abbey Farm. The stables and the cowshed had been replaced with modern buildings, but there was no change in the appearance of the old Abbey, which I was told was a listed building. I walked the path I had trod fifty years previously, but the Abbey was no longer an abode for workers — long-haired squatters had taken possession.

During Martinmas Week there had been a skeleton staff. This was universal practice on all farms. The horses had been neglected to some extent, and it was obvious that they had never felt the touch of a dandy-brush. "Elbow grease" would be necessary before the horses' coats were free of dust.

Ploughing stubble schedules to be sown with turnip seed in the Summer was the foreman's priority. If the last field was ploughed before Christmas he was satisfield. During December, we only saw the farmstead in daylight at noon, and sometimes plough wheels were turning before the dawn. Evening shadows were falling when we started the last turn round the rig.

Alf and I used to sing these words: "Now the day is over, night is drawing nigh," but this cut no ice with Fred Keast, and it was dark when we "loosed out." It may be difficult to believe today, but it was not unusual for a procession of plough horses to travel on a road in darkness without illumination of any kind.

On Christmas Eve we received a late meal consisting of a good helping of frumenty, a food made of boiled wheat and milk. I detested it, and given half a chance I would have given my portion to my pair of horses: they would have relished it. The next day our fare consisted of roast goose and plum pudding at noon, and in the evening boiled ham pies and Christmas cake. This day was our only official holiday: stock required attention, and if Christmas Day fell on a Sunday we did not get a day in lieu.

When we were preparing the horses for work in the early morning, Alf and myself were detailed to water them. We led them in pairs to a pond a short distance from the stable. During the week, when the horses were at work every day, we could lead them in halters. This was not the case on a Monday morning after they had had a weekend resting. In order to control the horses we had to put their blinkers on and thread the halter shanks through their respective bits.

When the ground was covered in snow, the horses snorted and reared up on their hind legs. It was essential to keep a short hold of the halters, and a few savage jerks on the bits soon brought the horses down to earth. This farm was no place for a lad on his first year off; he would not have been able to control the horses.

In the New Year a start was made to plough "awd seeds," a clover field which the sheep had grazed in the previous Summer. This was horse ploughing at its best. Every furrow was identical, plumb straight, and the ridges unbroken the length of a field. Woe betide the lad if he caused a slight bend from not holding his plough firmly in position. A field situated on the roadside was particularly open to criticism.

Some old men believed that pigs could see the wind. True or false, most horses detested it. They were reluctant to face a strong wind, and some were alarmed when it whistled through a hedge and disturbed the branches. One Monday morning, when the horses were full of high spirits as usual, there was a gale blowing. When Alf was turning his pair on the headland, he lost control of his startled horses due to his slack hold of the plough strings.

They galloped across the field and through a gate entry to a green lane and continued on to the farm. Because the surface was soft, the plough as a whole was undamaged, but a wheel and the coulter became loose and dropped off. Alf collected these as he followed behind, a very worried lad.

The horses had stopped in the stackyard, and when Alf arrived the foreman had them in hand. Alf expected to hear some harsh words, but instead the foreman said: "It weren't thy fault, lad. Osses are too fit by half."

It was important to ensure that a horse never had a second chance to gallop away, otherwise it would develop the habit and could never be trusted again. For this reason I was ordered to exchange one of my horses for one of Alf's runaways and keep strict control of the latter. This arrangement paid dividends, because a similar incident did not occur again, although there was a near miss at harvest.

On this occasion I was involved, and I had a very frightening experience. The corn was cut and sheaves produced with a binder. The sheaves were stooked and then carted home to be built into stacks and eventually threshed. Two binders were in operation, each one drawn by four horses. The foreman operated the first binder and Jim drove the team riding on the nearside pole-horse. The second binder was operated by Fred, and I drove the horses. I had orders not to encroach within approximately forty yards of the first binder.

When the sun was shining and the corn was swaying in a breeze which kept the horses cool, driving four horses yoked to a binder was one of the most pleasant aspects of horse-farming. However, this was not so on one particular afternoon when cutting was in progress. The signs of an approaching storm were plain to see, yet the foreman decided to risk another turn round the crop.

The first crack of thunder we heard was directly overhead. My horses literally jumped forward. They were difficult to hold in check and were gaining ground on the first binder. Fortunately, two stookers were on hand, and they clung to the farside horses' bits. Thanks to their help, I was able to stop the horses and an accident was averted.

By May we had threshed a stack of oats, and the yield was twenty quarters. The oats provided fodder for the horses throughout the Summer, harvest, and until wheat was sown at backend.

Two binders being operated at Hagg House Farm, Pickering, in 1923.

CHAPTER NINE

The sound of jet aircraft flying overhead reminds me of the noise created when a threshing machine was in operation. On a frosty morning the sound carried further than usual and could be heard over a wide area. We used to argue as we tried to pinpoint where threshing was taking place. The humming sound was pleasant to the ear, but working conditions were far from pleasant.

The only redeeming features were the two "looance tarms" served in the middle of the morning and in the afternoon. Except for these times and an hour at noon, threshing never stopped unless there was a breakdown.

We had twenty days threshing, and these were spread over the winter months. When fodder and straw was getting short, an oat stack was threshed and a barley stack too when the farmer required revenue. There was not a single job worth having on threshing day, but carrying corn was recognised as the most congenial.

"Carrying corn" involved carrying sacks a short distance and then climbing a dozen or so steps into the granary. The sacks were emptied, otherwise rats would have eaten their way into them and the sacks would have been ruined. When the stacks at the far side of the stackyard were threshed, the sacks were carted to the granary steps. At the top was a stone platform, and sold grain was loaded onto wagons from this point. This often took place before dawn, with the aid of stable lamps.

No farmer would consider hiring a horseman to be his wagoner if he was unable to "carry corn," and on a big farm thoddy was engaged to carry too. A man carried a sack across his shoulders so that the weight was not directly onto his back. At eighteen I carried barley and oats, the official weight of which were sixteen stones and twelve respectively. In the following year I carried wheat and filled the sacks to their full capacity, which reduced the number of journeys to the granary. 1919 was the last year I carried "caff."

The corn passed through two riddles which separated the smallest grain, which was called "inderends." The first grade was referred to as "foorends." There were four spouts at the end of the machine facing the engine. The foorends ran down the first two into sacks, tne inderends ran down the third, and rubbish and dust down the fourth. A slate was fixed above the spouts on which each sack carried away was recorded. This enabled a farmer to assess the yield.

There was only one mechanical lift on the farm, and it was operated by hand. Some called it a "hicking barrow," others a "winding-up barrow." It was mounted on two small, iron wheels, and a small platform was attached to it. When a sack was placed on this it could be raised to the required height by turning a handle. Then the platform was held in position with a

Portable steam engine used to power a threshing machine. It lacked traction and had to be pulled by horses.

Portable engine at work on a Wold farm before the turn of the century.

ratchet until the carrier pulled the sack down onto his shoulders. Dark or light, the machine began to hum at 7 a.m., and I have carried corn which was just a blur when it dropped down the spouts.

Matt, the local village blacksmith, owned a "threshing-set" and he provided a service for the majority of the farmers in the neighbourhood. No doubt he preferred being involved with his traction engine to shoeing horses. Fixed to the front of it was the figure of a rearing horse in brass. Matt polished this and the brass hoops which encircled the engine. When the threshing-set was travelling towards our farm and the sun was shining, the glistening brass-work could be seen from quite a distance.

Matt may have been proud of his engine, but it had no attraction for Alf and myself. We hated the sight of it. We carried the chaff from the machine to the "caff oose," the most detestable job experienced on a threshing day. Matt had the best job, for when he was not chasing us lads he spent most of his time sat on his engine, more often than not smoking his pipe. If a farmer complained, Matt would reply: "When thoo stops this awd engine from smoking Ah'll put me pipe oot."

The chaff was contained in hessian sheets, and when I had filled mine I twisted the four corners, then I flung the sheet over my left shoulder. As I walked away, all that could be seen of my back view was my cap, my legs below the knees, and my boots. Sometimes I felt a push from behind, but before I could turn round the culprit had disappeared.

To add to our contribution we were ordered to supply water to steam the engine. Matt would place a barrel near it, and we each took our turn and filled it with water carried in buckets from the pond. When the engine turned dry and the water had been sucked into the boiler, Matt came bouncing round to the machine to inform us that the barrel was empty.

On one occasion the yield was so heavy that it was nigh impossible for one lad to carry all the chaff, and I told Matt to fill the barrel himself. He picked up a stack-prod, a small hazel branch used in thatching, and chased me round the machine and corn stack. The third time round, Jim Atkins, one of the straw carriers, stuck his fork out in front of Matt and he tripped over it. He slunk away to his engine and never approached us again. The foreman took us in hand, and he also relieved us of the work involved when filling the barrel with water.

Nothing gave me more pleasure than the sight of the engine leaving the stackyard and trailing behind it the dusty, heat-creating machine. "Good riddance!" I used to shout as the red tail lamp disappeared into the dark night. Before we sat down to supper I stripped off to the waist and washed — there were no bath facilities in a farmhouse in those days.

It had been a day of rest for the horses. While we were slogging our guts out, they had spent the day in the stable, and they had left their mark too. After supper, before we could attend to the horses, we had to "muck oot."

Threshing at the end of a hard day on Charity Farm, Thornton Dale, 1920.

41

The stackyard was a shambles. The attractive corn-stack had disappeared, and in its place was an untidy straw-stack. The next morning the straw which had covered the steddle, the base for the corn-stack, and the obsolete thatch was carted into the foldyard. The straw would provide bedding for the bullocks and would eventually turn into manure.

There was also a heap of dust which had been discharged from the machine, and this was carried in sheets to the paddock, where it was spread thinly on the grass.

When we had finished our cleaning-up operation, the stackyard once again had a tidy appearance, the symbol of a well-managed farm. The standard was maintained until once again Matt turned up with his threshing set.

Winding up barrow.

CHAPTER TEN

Nowadays, with a combine, harvesting is soon over, and the only proof that such an event has taken place are the bales of new straw. When sheaves were produced and built into stacks, it was not practical to thresh them in one operation. In the first place there were no road vehicles available to transport the grain in bulk, and there were very few granaries able to hold more than the yield from two days' threshing. Storing the chaff or caff, essential horse fodder, from a complete threshing would have been a problem.

The stack containing the straw yield from one day's threshing required a base four times bigger than the one the corn-stack had been built on. The ground space for all the straw stacks could not have been found in the stackyard.

Carting the surplus straw into a field and burning it was out of the question too, for the whole yield was required as bedding for stock. This was eventually turned into manure, a farmer's main fertiliser. Cattle fed on linseed and cotton cakes, and meal obtained from ground cereals produced the richest manure. Evidence of this were the good crops of corn and roots taking shape in July. The land responded to cultivation, and produced far better results than land starved of manure.

After the harvest had been gathered at Abbey Farm, there were fourteen days threshing. A tremendous amount of manure acculumated during the Winter months, and it was never carted directly to a field and spread on the land. All the manure except that produced in the foldyard was turned over in five stages with the aid of muck forks. The five stages were as follows:

(a) Mucking out stables and the cow-house.

(b) Loading vehicles in the foldyard when leading was in progress.

(c) Teaming the manure into a midden.

(d) Loading vehicles from a midden.

(e) Spreading the manure on the land.

We were expected to make a midden as compact as a corn-stack. It was built in sections which were referred to as "desses." The first one would be about six feet square. When this reached a height out of reach of the teamer, he added another "dess." Eventually the horse manure created a combustion, and rubbish seeds among the straw perished.

When the time came to spread the manure on the land it was completely rotten. We always "mucked" for turnips, and when the manure had been ploughed in and the land cultivated, the manure had become part of the soil.

On small farms it was the custom to cart manure direct from the foldyard to a field and leave it in small heaps. These were not disturbed until the manure became rotten.

Creating heaps of manure to spread later.

On a frosty morning, when it was too hard to plough, we were pleased to hear the foreman say: "Gear yer osses for pluggin muck." The work was as good as any. Every muscle came into play, and a man's body generated heat. There was a break too when riding on a wagon to and from a midden.

Fred's wagon was the first to be loaded. We all got stuck in, and he was soon on his way to start a midden. The next wagon to be loaded was Jim's, then mine, followed by Alf's. Approximately identical loads were carried, and eventually, while one wagon was being loaded, another was travelling towards the midden. A third wagon was being teamed, and the fourth was on its way back to the foldyard.

There was a three-year-old in our stable which had never been yoked to a wagon, and muck-leading was as good a time as any to try it out. Fred yoked the horse at the far side of the pole. The foreman walked at the side of it and held a plough-string attached to the horse's bit, should this be required to hold it in check. Three journeys to the midden were sufficient to settle the horse down and dispense with the need for the foreman's efforts.

Tales of country life experienced during the nineteenth century were often told in our farmhouse when I was a boy. One concerned my grandfather's cousin, who at the age of eleven became a hired farm lad. He lived and worked on the same farm until his death, and remained a confirmed bachelor. In due course he passed through the different stages from "least lad" to foreman.

On his death bed his last wish for his remains to be conveyed on a wagon to the churchyard was granted. Just before his death he had sent for the wagoner and had given him this last order: "Yoke two black osses t wagon, an weh thoo leaves churchyard dee'ant fagit t bring them sheep nets yam." Apparently recently the sheep had eaten off a field of turnips adjacent to the churchyard. When the sheep had been removed to another field, a few nets had been left behind.

No one could accuse old-time farm foremen of "carrying coals to Newcastle": their organising ability was second to none. A farm foreman had problems unknown to this counterpart in industry, whose work was mainly repetition. Indifferent weather conditions did not interfere with production, as was often the case on a farm. When corn sowing was in progress a night's rain cancelled the operation the following morning, until moisture dried out of the land. At short notice a foreman had to organise alternative work for his men.

Ex-wagoners were the most successful foremen. Their knowledge and experience enabled them to get the best results from their men and the horses. They never interfered with the work in the stable, and rarely entered one except when a sick or lame horse required attention.

According to one tale told by my grandfather, a shepherd he knew tried his hand at being a foreman. The routine he practised meant that he was continually at loggerheads with the respective wagoners, and one left before March was out. His demand to be paid up to date was refused until he threatened: "Thas bin yar chap hung fa modda fra this village, and thal bi another if Ah disunt git mi money!"

CHAPTER ELEVEN

The achievements of yesterday's farm foremen are above criticism: their services were indispensable on a large farm. They organised the labour force and were responsible for cultivation, the sowing and harvesting of crops, and also for the maintenance of the harnesses, tools, vehicles and implements. It was the foreman who decided when and which horses required new shoes.

The two farms High and Low Gardham, at Cherry Burton, comprised 1050 acres and were recognised as two of the best barley farms on the Yorkshire Wolds. From 1882 until 1903 they were farmed as one unit under the same management, and after harvest there were sixty days of threshing. The stacks were thatched: forty containing barley sheaves had priority, followed by oats and wheat. 400 ewes and 600 hog-sheep were wintered on turnips, and 200 bullocks were fed for beef in the foldyards.

There were thirty-two working horses plus two allotted to the herdsmen to lead turnips from a field. Ten horsemen were hired, as well as two herdsmen, four shepherds and five labourers, all of them single men. The foreman's house where they lived was a busy place, with twenty-one men and lads sitting down to meals when the bell rang. The six tied cottages were occupied by the head shepherd, the head herdsman, three labourers and a blacksmith. When the last of the fat sheep and bullocks had been sold in Spring, all the labour force came under the supervision of the foreman.

Each horse required a halter, blinkers, collar and a pair of traces attached to a hemp back-band. There were five sets of wagon harness, each one consisting of four pairs of special traces attached to leather back-bands, four belly-bands, two breechings and a riding saddle, also sufficient pairs of reins, fifteen pairs of plough strings and six cart saddles, fifteen cobble trees and thirty swingletrees. Twelve wagons and six carts were available for use.

It is difficult to estimate the number of implements required on a farm of this size, but included in the list were harrows, drags, shims, rollers, corn and turnip seed drills, horse-rakes, and four corn reapers, as well as fifteen ploughs.

All the straw was required for fodder or bedding, and owing to the amount of feeding stuffs used, rich straw was produced. Every week the wagoner visited the cake mill Barkers of Beverley and brought three ton loads of feeding cakes to the farm. When he had finished loading his wagon, he was presented with a voucher which entitled him to obtain a free pint of beer at the Fleece Inn.

I am indebted to an old friend who was the wagoner at Gardham in 1901 for the following narrative.

"In Winter I used to spend more time on the roads driving four horses yoked to a wagon than I did ploughing. It was usually 6.00 a.m. when I passed through Cherry Burton on my way to Beverley. It was often dark and no lamps were carried. We had our own portable engine threshing set, and sometimes we had a fortnight's threshing at one time. The barley passed down the spouts into railway sacks. These were weighed and delivered to Cherry Burton station and put on rail.

"It was a grand sight to see five wagons loaded with sacks of corn, each one drawn by four horses, their tails plaited with ribbons and polished brasses attached to the harness. Some of the fields were 100 acres, and when a corn seed drill had been a turn about in one, an acre had been sown. One of the drills was known as a 'steerage drill' and three men were required to operate it.

"The four horses yoked to it were driven in the same manner as when yoked to a wagon. One man walked by the side of the drill and kept it to the correct mark by means of a steering wheel. When an acre was sown, a bell attached to the drill rang, and this occurred thirty times each day.

"When a Mr Spillman took possession of the farms on Lady Day 1903 he introduced a new fashion in corn drills: these were two-horse pole drills which registered each acre as it was completed, and they were reasonably accurate. The labour force was reduced to one. A wagoner could drive his pair of horses yoked to the drill and also operate it. Later, the two-furrow plough was introduced, and one man with a team of three horses turned over as many furrows in a day as two men and their respective pairs of horses."

Today, Gardham is completely mechanised, and machines literally do the work. The organisation required is practically nil when compared to that practised when horses were the only power available to work the land. The old-time farm foremen were a special breed, and their knowledge and ability could not be obtained by reading and studying.

CHAPTER TWELVE

Careful handling and consideration for a team's workload saved horseflesh, but feeding had priority. Indeed, it was so important that a wagoner would not allow a lad to give a horse a feed without permission. Draymen employed by the railway companies were not allowed to feed their horses: a stable-man was responsible for their keep.

The fodder consisted of rolled oats, bran, and chopped hay. Each horse, regardless of its appetite, received the same amount en bloc morning, noon or night — a procedure I never practised when employed as a farm wagoner.

The times spent loading or teaming a dray were rest periods for the horse. This did not, however, apply to a team of farm horses yoked to an implement: they were never allowed to stop unless it was necessary.

At the Hirings held in Scarborough in 1925 Bill Grice, the foreman at Wold Farm, West Heslerton, hired me to be the wagoner. In the Spring I drilled twenty acres of corn in one day with a pair of horses. This would not have been possible if the horses had been in poor condition. During my hiring days I came across, to coin a phrase, horses who would get fat on nowt. This was not the case with Willie Hall's horses at Wold Farm: they ate their heads off, yet had a lean appearance. It was possible to change their image if you had the knowledge and could obtain special fodder.

A mixture of oats and chaff, which was the horses' staple diet, was not sufficient. Barley chaff was not ideal fodder, for the horns among it often formed a wad at the back of the horse's mouth. If this was not removed in time a sore would develop. On a Wold farm, the main crop was barley, and there was no alternative but to mix the chaff with oat or wheat chaff. This neutralised the horns to some extent, yet every day I examined my horses' mouths to ensure that no barley had lodged in them.

The mixture, referred to as a feed, was contained in a small sieve, and this enabled me to remove the dust from the chaff. Regardless of this, some horses with particularly sensitive noses were able to separate the dust which was left in the crib.

The number of feeds each horse received in one session depended on its appetite. Oats were the ideal fodder for horses because they did not swell when subject to moisture. If wheat or barley in a natural state was fed to a horse, the grain would swell in its body and the horse was at high risk from an attack of colic, which was painful and often fatal.

I knew a wagoner who fed his horses with wheat in its raw state, and this resulted in the death of three of them. This would not have happened if he had previously treated the grain in a manner which would have caused it to swell. "Creaded" was the name given to grain in this state, and a double handful among a horse's last feed at night soon improved its condition.

To my knowledge this practice was strictly forbidden by the majority of farmers. I obtained a supply on the sly. It was contained in a small bag which I buried in the foldyard where there was sufficient moisture. When I recovered it, the grain was sprouted, and the horse relished it in this state. I used to raid the cake-house too, for a handful of crushed linseed given to each horse at night left its mark. The extra gloss on their skins was the evidence. One farmer who employed me remarked: "A wagoner is no good if he doesn't pinch extra grub for his horses."

The old saying: "A poor farmer keeps poor horses" was true. No doubt when a wagoner arrived after Martinmas Week, a stranger onto the farm, he would find the granary door locked and the oats rationed below the recognised amount. A horse at work on the land during the Winter required a stone each day, increased by a half a stone in the Spring.

When a farmer was niggardly in this respect, most wagoners would go to any lengths to increase the horses' rations. On a farm where the granary had been built above the stable, it was not an unusual practice for a feeder to bore a hole in the floor underneath a heap of oats. When the plug was removed, an additional supply was available.

During the Winter months there were occasions when a heavy fall of snow or a series of hard frosts held up ploughing. When such a situation occurred, I used to reduce their ration of oats, otherwise the lack of exercise might cause grease in a horse's hind legs, which was an irritable complaint. It was essential that horses should have a keen appetite when ploughing re-started. If they had been fed to their full capacity most likely several would be off their grub at the end of the day. The reason was a mystery to me. I measured the oats in an old, worn pie dish, and I developed a sixth sense regarding the amount each horse required.

Today the farm wagoners' concern for their horses' welfare may be difficult to understand, but they certainly had real affection for their teams. There was no pleasure in working sluggish horses or pride in driving four horses in poor spirits yoked to a wagon.

When a goods yards was full of farm vehicles, the horses in their turn were scrutinised by different wagoners. One whose horses were in poor condition could expect to hear the following remark: "Why disunt thoo pinch some extra grub for thy 'osses?"

Within two months of my arrival at Wold Farm, the horses had a changed appearance. Their ribs and backbones were well covered with flesh. One day Bill Grice, the foreman, remarked: "Our 'osses ev niva looked si weal!"

A wagoner's pair in peak condition, "round as barrels."

CHAPTER THIRTEEN

1919 was the first complete year of peace, and the inflated prices farmers had obtained for their produce and stock during the war continued. There was a steady return of country men who had served during the war, and once again farmers were able to obtain the services of adult horsemen. "Toonies" who had been directed to work on the land were delighted to leave the farms for the bright lights.

In March a law was passed which reduced working hours each day from eleven to nine, except on a Saturday, when for the first time normal work finished at noon. Getting rid of fifteen working hours each week was remarkable, but it was the holiday on Saturday afternoons which were the most beneficial.

As might be expected, farmers were not pleased with their men's improved working conditions, and worse was to follow: 1919 turned out to be the last year of prosperity for farmers. The following year prices began to fall — an indication of the economic depression which was to continue until the outbreak of the Second World War in 1939.

When I hear the ballad "Bill's across the meadow," I am reminded of a little church which nestled in a valley on the Wolds. The church was some distance from the village and overlooking it on a hillside was a grass field. It belonged to the farm where I was employed as the "third lad" in 1920. The pasture was adjacent to the farside boundary.

On fine Sunday evenings in the Summer, Dick Dale, the wagoner, and myself walked down a green lane viewing the crops growing in fields on either side. Particular notice was taken of the turnip rows. When sowing the seed there had been keen competition between us to see which one could lead the drill-horse to create the straightest rows.

Three horses yoked to a drill, 1920.

It was usually church time when we arrived at the pasture, and as we looked over the gate we could see the villagers wending their way to attend the evening service. While the peal of bells could be heard loud and clear across the valley, young unbroken horses grazed in the pasture, and we discussed their good and bad points.

Our next visit was to another pasture where the working horses grazed to ensure that none of them had suffered an injury. On one visit we had found a horse lame. Its nearside hind shoe had worked loose and turned on its foot, and the toe-clip had penetrated the foot. Immediate treatment was required or the affected part may have become inflamed.

There were grey, black and brown horses in the field, and nearer home three mares and their foals grazed in a paddock. My pair of plough horses, Captain and Boxer, were black, my favourite colour for a horse. I preferred a name with two syllables, because if a horse was not pulling its weight, the second syllable could be stressed and the horse usually reacted favourably.

I recall with pleasure these by-gone pleasant Sunday evening strolls, and also the 6 a.m. walks to a pasture during the week to collect the horses. As I was putting the halter on one of my pair, the other would join me. No doubt it did not intend being left behind. Breathing the pure, fresh air in the early morning and the work involved in preparing the horses for the day ahead ensured that I ate a hearty breakfast.

The Grange was a typical Wold farm of about 400 acres, with fifteen working horses. The hired horsemen consisted of Jim Dale, the foreman, his brother, Dick, myself and our respective lads. Bob Varey was the fourth lad, and he looked after three horses. Jim had served throughout the war with Sir Mark Sykes's Wagoners Reserves and had returned home with barely a scratch.

We lived in the farmhouse and sat down to meals prepared by the servant girl. She was hired too and had to wait until Martinmas Day for her wages. Breakfast was over by 7 a.m., and on a Monday as we were leaving the kitchen she was hard at work washing clothes in an outhouse.

During the Winter we often — too often — had roast rabbit for dinner. A large dish appeared on the table conspicuous for the absence of rabbits' legs, which had been served to the farmer and his family. The servant girl was not to blame, but one day Bob swore at her and said: "I've never seen so many two-headed rabbits in my life!"

His remark was heard in the next room, and consequently there was a confrontation between master and man which resulted in Bob being offered his wages to date — which he accepted. He packed his box with his belongings and carried it home. His father was the shepherd on the next farm and lived in a tied cottage. Farm workers did not contribute towards unemployment insurance and Bob was unable to draw the dole during the Winter. It was Spring before he managed to obtain another place.

CHAPTER FOURTEEN

Every Thursday night in January until the end of March, Dick and myself biked to the village of Fridaythorpe to attend dance classes. They were held in the school from 8.00 p.m. until 10.00 p.m. The admission fee was sixpence, and music was provided by a honky-tonk piano. We had little opportunity to show our steps at dances, for those held in villages were few and far between. In later years they became more popular, and I benefitted from the classes I had attended.

Before the end of January days were lengthening, and this meant more time at work in the fields, which continued in the afternoons until daylight faded. We were well forward with our work: we had finished ploughing the old clover fields, and a start had been made to plough the land cleared of turnips. This was completed in the first two weeks of February, except for the last beak of turnips feeding the sheep.

Jim had broken in a pair of two-year-old horses, and when possible had gone to plough with us. He had taken the lead as we expected, and no time was lost. His next priority was "quartering" the ploughed stubble fields scheduled to be sown with turnip seed.

The fine Spring enabled us to complete the sowing of oats and barley in March. Bank holidays were not recognised on farms, and it was work as usual on Easter Monday, but Good Friday was a mystery regarding the number of hours we would have to work. There was a good chance of it being a holiday if good progress had been made or if wet weather held up sowing. However, some farmers would allow their men a full day's holiday regardless, others half a day. It was not unusual for a farmer who was a churchman to say to his men: "If you attend church in the morning you can have the afternoon off."

There were no concessions in this respect on one farm where in later years I was the wagoner. I recall being envious of walkers dressed in their Sunday best as they passed the field where I was drilling corn. Lambing time was over and the shepherd was relieved of his nightly vigils. He had moved his flock from a home pasture to a young clover field. We had got rid of his ewes' melancholy lamentations and the lambs' bleatings heard when they had lost sight of their mothers.

There were other arrivals due — in my eyes special and more important too. The three mares, Bonny, Topper and Darling, were so heavy that they could only walk slowly and would eventually produce their foals. Bonny, otherwise gentle, was so jealous of her foal that she showed a vicious streak. She bared her teeth and I had to keep an eye on her in the initial stages when I entered the loose box.

Nothing was too good for a mare after she had foaled. For several days she was given lukewarm water to drink and a warm bran mash which was mixed in with a feed. Each mare was allowed ten days rest in order to recuperate. No farm animal's offspring created more interest than a new-born foal. The majority of foals were born during the night, and the following morning each foal had a stream of visitors. Everybody on the farm, including the missus and her servant, were prompted to have a peep at it through the loose box door.

After several weeks a foal began to cast its original coat, and when this was completed the foal was a different colour. There were discussions in the stable regarding this, and also, of course, the foal's good and bad points. If a mare died when foaling there was gloom on the farm, especially if the foal was lost too. A foal which lost its mother when it was several weeks old had the best chance of survival. It was bottle fed on cow's milk, which was not as rich in sugar as a mare's milk. The foal became a pet, and for this reason was referred to as a "pet foal."

When a pet foal was two years old and in the process of being broken in, there were problems for, to coin a phrase, the horse had "too much off." It was essential to create a soft cushion in a horse's mouth in which a bit would be placed. Otherwise the horse would not respond when pressure was put on the bit with a pair of reins.

To accomplish this a horse was backed into a stall and each bit ring was connected to the respective pillar with an appropriate length of plough string. Due to champing the outsize bit, the horse's mouth eventually became tender. One which had been a pet foal was reluctant to do this unless it was persuaded through rough treatment. A horse of this nature could not be described as being "handy" and one of our horses was a typical example.

The first Winter of its life it had lived rough among cattle in the foldyard. It had received a feed of corn morning and night, and at noon had eaten turnips and hay — the cattle fodder. When the herdsman was "foddering up" he carried the turnips contained in a scuttle on his left shoulder and he had to keep an eye on the foal. Given half a chance it would have slunk up behind him, grabbed the spare handle with its teeth, and pulled the scuttle off his shoulder.

When the foreman had broken "Duke" he had done his best, but the horse was nobody's favourite, and a lad was reluctant to accept it as one of his pair of plough horses. It was useless when yoked between the shafts of a cart. It jibbed, and if roughly treated reared on its hind legs.

My grandfather would never allow me to pet a foal. "The less they are handled until the time comes to break them in the better," he used to say. My uncle's foals were weaned when the corn was ready to harvest and most likely at some future date they would work at their mother's side, but neither of the animals would recognise each other.

Pair of mares, mother and daughter – latter nearer camera.

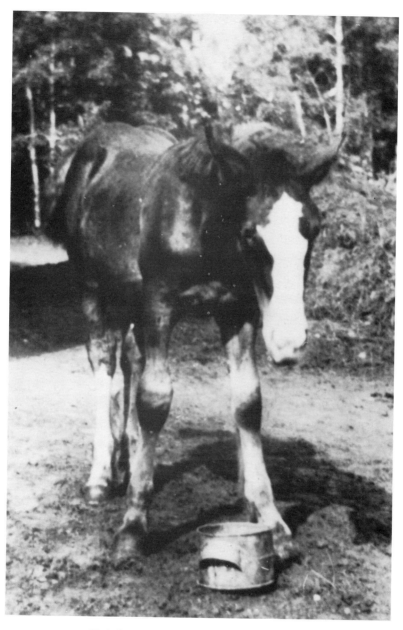

Typical pet foal, which lost its mother at six weeks.

57

CHAPTER FIFTEEN

The cuckoo had returned from overseas, and its call was welcome as it signified that warmer weather was on the way. Once again grass was springing into life, and the time was drawing near when the horses would be turned out to sleep in the pasture. After being tied down to horse-keeping during the Winter, free weekends were welcomed. I was able to bike home — my first visit since I had arrived at this farm, and I certainly appreciated work finishing at noon on a Saturday.

The horses were tired of dry fodder and were as keen to taste the luscious grass as we were to turn them out. Grass was referred to as "doctor-green." A horse which had lost its appetite soon regained it, and minor complaints such as "grease" on a horse's hind legs were cured.

The first week in April Will Haig called at the farm with his stallion and would continue his visits until he was sure the three mares were in foal again.

We had finished quartering and had made a start to cultivate a field to be sown with swede turnip seeds. The land was dragged and rolled alternately, which reduced the size of the clots and released the weeds which the sun eventually killed. Getting rid of the wicks was the most difficult task. When the weather was fine we could burn them on the land, otherwise they had to be carted off. If good results were to be obtained it was essential to complete turnip sowing before the end of June.

The horses worked throughout the Summer. When the sun was blazing they were lathered with sweat. Consequently they lost condition, especially the three-year-olds and the mares with foals at foot. Once the turnip sowing was completed all the horses were able to enjoy a well-earned rest except two, which were required to pull a scruffler.

Dick and myself, because we did not require horses, could stay in bed an extra half hour, but the two lads were unlucky in this respect. They used the scrufflers, and each one had his special horse, one which would walk between the rows and never put a foot on a plant. The lads had to bring the horses into the stable at the usual time and prepare them for work before breakfast.

A scruffler was the smallest horse-drawn implement on the farm, yet it was essential for the production of turnips. The oblong frame could be adjusted to coincide with the width between the rows. Attached to each side was an L-shaped knife set at a backward angle to allow the soil to pass between it. The knives cut the weeds growing between the rows, and there were no problems when the land was dry. Otherwise, the weeds stuck to the knives, and if they were not cleaned continually, the soil accumulated. This spread onto the plants and hoeing became difficult.

At the front of the scrufflier was a small iron wheel and a hook to which a swingle-tree could be attached. The two handles fixed to the frame enabled a horseman to hold the implement in position. Scruffling was not the simple job it looked. If it was not held on an even keel the scruffler would veer to one side. Plants would be knocked up, and permanent gaps in a row would result.

Operating a scruffler was a monotonous affair, yet I preferred it to hoeing turnips. When I was the wagoner's lad at Abbey Farm, thoddy's lad and myself used to couple our horse together and scruffle every other row. We could talk as we crossed the field together. The foreman turned a blind eye — he was only concerned when he saw us stopped.

In July turnip hoeing was the order of the day, and we followed each other in the following order: the foreman, wagoner, myself, the shepherds, two labourers and the beastman brought up the rear. Single plants were left seven inches apart and a certain amount of soil was drawn into the middle of the row. This created a ridge and caused the plants to droop. When they had recovered, scruffling continued. This levelled the soil and caused it to spread back among the plants.

When we were hoeing in one particular field we had a good view of the Vale of York. The different colours of the crops growing in the fields resembled a patchwork quilt. At this time of the year the corn was ripening and the leaves of root crops were gradually covering the brown earth with various colours of green. Today, instead of fields there are large areas barren of trees and hedges and the scene is far less attractive.

Several airships were based at a village called Howden some twenty miles away, and on a clear day I have seen one rise from the ground no bigger than a toy balloon to the naked eye.

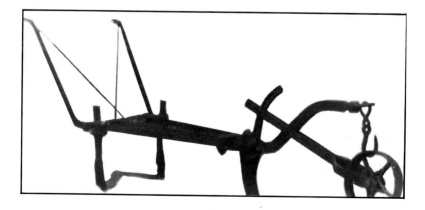

A scruffler.

59

CHAPTER SIXTEEN

The nearest town to Grange Farm was Pocklington, situated at the foot of the Wolds. It was linked to Beverley and York by rail and was a typical Yorkshire market town. It served a farming community covering a large area, including a number of Wold farmers.

Traders and tradesmen had been established for generations, and businesses had been handed down from father to son. They relied upon farmers and their workers for a large percentage of their business. Market Day was a busy day for them as was Saturday night, when the shops were open and the centre of the town full of young people. The majority were from the surrounding farms. When the Picture House opened, where silent films were shown, the street was soon deserted.

I left my bike in one of the yards belonging to a public house when I visited the town. In 1916 it became compulsory by law to have a red rear-light on a bike — previously only a paraffin lamp was carried. I converted mine into a rear-lamp when carbide lamps appeared in the shops. These cost between 5/- and 7/6 and a more elaborate one could be bought for 17/6. The illumination was a great improvement when compared to that obtained from a paraffin lamp.

Carbide was placed in a container in the bottom part of the lamp, and a vessel in the top half was filled with water. When in use, drops dripped onto the carbide, and the supply could be regulated by means of a thumb screw. This mixture created a gas which passed through a tube which supplied a burner behind the glass face of the lamp. When the gas was ignited a light appeared, but too much water turned the carbide into paste and then no gas was produced.

I never heard of a bike being stolen, but sometimes a lad found the carbide in his lamp had been flooded with water. I had this trick played on me one night and I had to ride home without a head-light. I was caught, and the result was a fine of 5/-. I found this difficult to understand, because whenever I had passed the same policeman driving four horses yoked to a wagon without lights he had turned a blind eye. When I pointed this out to him he replied: "It's a different matter when you are at work." He never caught me again for on future occasions I carried a spare supply of carbide in a tin.

The Beverley-York railway passed through Pocklington, and farm carts and wagons could often be seen going to or leaving the station. Wagons came down from the Wolds carrying fifteen quarters of barley. The horses' tails had been plaited with ribbons, and attached to their harnesses were highly polished brasses.

When the horses entered the town they raised their heads high and pricked up their ears. The close proximity of houses and shops was

60

something they only experienced occasionally. Old hands who had retired to live in the town stood and admired the horses. No doubt their thoughts were of bygone days when they had driven a team yoked to a wagon through the town.

Every year thousands of tons were despatched to and from the goods yard at Pocklington. Most of this was the farmers' corn and hay which had been sold. One day when Dick and myself, each with a wagon, arrived at the goods yard we found it full of farm vehicles. We had to queue outside and wait our turn to enter.

When we had left the town behind, our wagons loaded with coal, there was a long haul uphill for the horses. They worked in harmony, and each horse pulled its weight at a steady pace which never varied. Halfway up the hill the road levelled out a short distance sufficient for the wagon to remain stationary when we stopped the horses. While they had a short rest we sat on the grass verge. The chance of a motor vehicle bearing down upon us was practically nil.

Every year an Agricultural Show was held at Pocklington and it was well supported. The horses and cattle on the farms in this area were as good as any found in the country, and exhibits came from near and far. The heavy horses created the most interest, and judging continued through the day to music played by the British Oil and Cake Mills band from Hull. Sports were held in the evening and there were cups and medals to be won. Musical chairs was played by horses and riders to the music played by the band. It also provided the music for the dance which took place in the marquee later. The largest cup was presented to the winning tug of war team. This was filled with beer or spirits several times during the night.

The Show was strictly related to agriculture — the judging of stock, poultry and produce. Only the few up-to-date implements on view were connected to the commercial world. The judges were chosen from well-known horse dealers who, on the hottest days, were immaculate in their hard hats, breeches, black leggings, and boots.

The main breeds involved were Shires, Clydesdales, Hunters and Hackneys. Brood mares were shown with or without their foals. There were classes for foals and for every age group from one to five-year-olds. There was a cup for the owner of the horse judged to be the best in the Show, and finally the pairs of decorated plough horses geared to pull a cart were judged.

Although the buckles and the undersides of straps were scrutinised, it was a problem judging the winners. When the five-year-old Shires were being exhibited the judges looked for one standing seventeen hands on good legs, big sound feet, large knees and hocks, a short back and wide quarters. A loose-limbed horse with a good swinging gait was sure to catch the judge's eye.

Agricultural shows were organised in every market town and also in many large villages each year. These took place in July and early August before the harvest was ready. The majority of farmers allowed their men a day off in order to attend the local show.

Preparations began a few weeks before the actual date and were carried out voluntarily by the hired horsemen. A judge never gave a horse in poor condition a second glance, and those selected were only worked when it was essential. The horses were brought into the stable in the evenings, groomed, and given a feed of corn. Their manes and tails were combed and their legs washed until they reached peak condition. The night before the show they were completely washed and kept in the stable overnight. Harness and brasses were continually cleaned and polished. Farmers who exhibited their horses every year owned special harnesses only brought out of storage on this and similar occasions.

On the morning of the show the horses received their final grooming. Their manes and tails were plaited with ribbons and other decorations were attached. Only experts could plait to show ring standards, and the reward for their services were the pints of beer they were treated to. There were no motor transport vehicles in which the horses could be conveyed. A pair was coupled together and driven to the show field and a single horse was led.

Wagoners pinned their faith on the five-year-olds which had been schooled to the standard required by town firms. When the time came for a farmer to sell a prize-winner he could obtain a price above the average. Farmers owed the success of their horses to their hired horsemen, but very few allowed them to keep the prize money. This would not have compensated them for the hours they spent — in their own time — preparing the horses. In an era when there were no annual holidays for farm workers, attending a local show was an occasion to look forward to.

Since the decline of farm horses, Agricultural Shows are no longer held in villages and a pleasant rural event has disappeared. There are retired countrymen who can recall a sunny day when they paraded a horse round a show ring or watched the various classes being judged. Perhaps these memories are some compensation for the holidays they were denied in their younger days.

CHAPTER SEVENTEEN

A motor car travelling on the Wold roads was a rare sight, and people could walk along them without apprehension. It was not unusual to see tramps walking aimlessly on their way, their place of origin a mystery. Most of them travelled up and down the country, but a few never left the Wolds. They spent the winter in institutions and returned to their wanderings in the spring.

The majority of these Wold tramps were prepared to work for any favours they received. Odd ones were well-educated and it was easy to tell by their accents that they did not belong to the farming fraternity. Such a one was "Picture-frame Dick." He carried a certain amount of haberdashery and some pictures which he peddled on his way. Each picture illustrated a biblical scene with the verse of a well-known hymn printed underneath it.

How he came by his nickname was a mystery, because his pictures were not framed! Dick received a cordial welcome from the women who lived on the farms he visited, especially if he had news of their relatives who lived in another area. He ensured that he arrived at our farm at noon, because he knew he would be invited to sit down to a meal at our table. After Dick had completed his business in the house, he visited the stable, but the reception he received was not always friendly.

If Martinmas was drawing near, hired lads were as hard up as he was, and he risked being thrown out of the stable. Otherwise he displayed his pictures on the corn bin lid, but he had little chance of selling one. He offered to sell us cotton boot-laces, but they were useless for hobnailed boots, which required leather laces.

He traded in horses brasses, and if these could have talked, what tales they could have told. I own a pair of face pieces I bought from Dick for a shilling, and one is slightly bent. One horse of mine had developed the habit of slipping its halter during the night. It took a delight in knocking the harness off the wooden pegs protruding from the walls. One morning when I entered the stable I found that the horse had trodden on the blinkers to which the brass was attached and it had bent under its feet.

During the summer, donkeys carrying riders on the sands were a common sight. When the holiday season came to an end, owners visited farms in order to obtain winter homes for their donkeys until they required them again. Most farmers, especially those with a young family, were willing to accept one. When the time came for the donkeys to be collected, they were in better condition than when they had first arrived.

On a farm where sheep were wintered on turnips a donkey certainly earned its keep. Turnips fed to sheep were put through a cutter and sliced into large chips. It was hard work for a shepherd pulling this machine between the heaps of turnips, especially when the land was soft. It was not difficult to train a donkey to do this work and it was provided with a collar and a pair of traces. Every morning it was taken to the sheepfold where it remained all day and at noon it was fed on hay. When the shepherd arrived home at night he left the donkey in a shed. He knew a horse-lad would water and groom it and give it a feed of "caff an coo-an" (chaff and oats).

Who was responsible for our donkey's antics I never knew, but when its owner realised that no one could ride it, he returned it. When he was offered a fiver — a good price for a donkey in those days — he accepted it. The donkey had a good life grazing in the paddock during the summer instead of carrying riders on the sand. In the winter when it was yoked to the cutter, the shepherd could not praise the donkey too highly. No doubt it knew which side its bread was buttered.

On the fringe of our furthest boundary was a fold-yard surrounded by a barn and loose boxes. In the winter the latter provided shelter for the young unbroken horses and store cattle were kept in the fold-yard. At harvest corn gathered from nearby fields was stacked near the fold-yard. When the stacks were threshed the straw yield provided fodder or bedding for the stock and it was eventually turned into manure.

After we had finished hoeing turnips we were sent with our horses and wagons to clean out the fold-yard. The manure was spread on a clover field which would be sown with wheat at backend. At noon we unyoked the horses, stripped them, and allowed them to graze in a paddock. The master brought our dinners by horse and trap.

When we had eaten we could lie in the sun until the horses were required at 1.00 p.m. There was entertainment too provided by the lads and the donkey. Regardless of the times they tried to ride it they were unseated.

The land was dry and it was not hard work for a pair of horses to pull a wagon loaded with manure. Except for the two required to pull the scrufflers, the horses had not worked since June. The three and four-year-olds had grown and filled out, and the older horses had become fat and lazy. They were in soft condition and the exercise experienced when muck-leading prepared the horses for harvest when they would be subjected to the hard work of pulling binders.

CHAPTER EIGHTEEN

The date for the harvest cannot be arranged before the corn is ripe, because this depends on the weather, which plays a vital role throughout the year. On the Wolds when it had been seasonable the corn was ready to harvest the first week in August. It was gathered in before the end of September unless the weather was exceptionally wet.

Today, with the aid of a combine, the same amount of corn is cut and threshed in a matter of days. Grain can be dried by artificial means, and farmers are not subject to the anxiety that they were in the past when they had to rely on sun and wind to dry the corn. When the weather was favourable harvesting was a pleasure in spite of the long days and the hard work involved. Everybody worked full out to gather the corn into the stackyard. A successful harvest guaranteed the farming community a living for the following year.

Before a binder was taken into a field, an area near the gate was mown with a scythe and the corn was gathered and tied to form sheaves. An area round the outside of the crop was also cleared to create a path for the horses to walk. Three harvesters worked as a team — the mower followed by the gatherer, then a "least lad" whose job it was to make the corn bands and fasten them round the sheaves. The only sounds audible were those made when the corn came into contact with the sharp blade. Sometimes there was a rustle in the hedge bottom when a rabbit scuttled to safety.

Before I left school, I followed the mower and my Uncle Bill, who was the gatherer. When the crop was heavy, more sheaves were produced and I was unable to keep pace with them. Gradually the row of untied sheaves lengthened until they decided to down tools and helped me, Bill remarking jovially: "Thoos a bit slow for a youngun!"

Working between the long corn and hedge row when a mist hung over the ground restricted our view. I used to imagine we were in a world of our own. While this work, known as "opening out," was taking place, the horses were resting in the stable and feeding on tares. When the dew had dried off the corn their day's work began.

Cutting continued — weather permitting — until 7.00 p.m. When the horses arrived home they were fed and groomed before being turned out. One night I was climbing into bed when I remembered the horses were still in the stable. This meant getting dressed in order to turn them out.

Although hired workers did not benefit from the extra hours they worked, the married men were hired for a month for a sum of money above their weekly rate. When the binders were in operation they stooked the sheaves. On the Wolds there were swarms of rabbits. In the Spring they fed off the young corn and large areas were laid bare. During the Summer the rabbits invaded the corn crops.

"Opening out" at harvest. Creating a path round a crop for horses to walk.

66

Binder and horses at work in evening shadows.

When driving a team yoked to a binder I had a good view of the corn from the saddle horse's back. A rabbit running towards the centre, startled by the machine, was plain to see. If cutting was not completed the same day the rabbits would leave the remaining corn during the night. Otherwise they stayed until a narrow strip was left.

Meanwhile the stookers, armed with sticks, had surrounded the area. The laid sheaves hindered the rabbits' escape and they were fair game. Each stooker was allowed to keep a couple and us hired lads who lived in could expect rabbit pie for dinner the next day.

Leading the sheaves home was the climax to the cutting and stooking was the most satisfying and interesting of all harvest operations. Lads competed to see which one could make the best shaped load, although it disappeared into a stack soon after it arrived at the stackyard. The ends of a load here higher than the middle and were made narrower until one row of sheaves completed it. The last sheaf placed on each end was referred to as a "wee-a-tie."

Stacks began to take shape and space in the stackyard disappeared. Wheat, barley and oat stacks were built on "steddles" (bases) positioned in the same place every year. These received a thick covering of straw to protect the bottom sheaves from the damp ground.

Oats and barley required for seed in the Spring were stacked at the far side of the stackyard. These and a stack of oats to provide fodder for horses in the Summer were threshed last.

One of the most important harvest jobs was stacking sheaves of corn. Failure to build a stack which was weatherproof resulted in a loss for a farmer. When threshing took place, any damp grain could not be separated completely from the rest, which also became affected. In this condition it would not sell, and when ground into meal was poor fodder for cattle or pigs.

A farmer would not consider a man to be his foreman if he was unable to stack. On a Wolds farm 300 acres or more, the wagoner was expected to be able to stack. If he had never built one before he was given the chance to have a go. More than likely his efforts would be successful, for in previous years when teaming loads of sheaves, he had noticed and remembered the procedure practised by the stacker. The foreman and wagoner each stacked on end and met half-way — a case of the master keeping an eye on his pupil.

Two loads arrived at the stack together, and while these were being teamed, two more were being loaded in the field. When the weather was favourable, it was remarkable how soon the sheaves were transformed into stacks. They were positioned in rows with sufficient space between them for a threshing set to operate. Gradually, as the days passed, the stackyard began to fill up.

Rain was the bogey, and when leading operations were held up, one

Field of stook rows.

Typical stackyard scene.

70

alternative job was "drawing straw" required for thatching the stacks. Wheat straw was always used as it was the most substantial. It was stripped of the foliage and the short lengths were removed before it was tied up in bundles. When leading was in progress time used to fly, but this was not the case when "drawing straw." The hours were long and dreary and there were times when I used to think the day's work would never end.

Building a stack was a remarkable achievement because it took place under the stacker's feet. My grandfather could complete a stack and not return to ground level except for his meals. When I was building one I came down at every opportunity to ensure that it was not leaning to one side.

Leading continued until it was too dark to see. It was not unusual for a lad when leaving a field with his last load to realise that his wagon-wheel had made contact with a gate-post. Nine times out of ten this broke off at ground level. I was not surprised when I heard a lad brag: "Ah yance knocked bee-ath posts doon at yar go," because this did happen occasionally.

While horses were being stripped and turned out to grass, last loads and the stack were sheeted down. After supper it was bed-time, but there was one concession: harvesting was halted at 6.00 p.m. on a Saturday. If no time was lost we could bike to the local picture house for the second showing.

CHAPTER NINETEEN

Before 1930 farmers produced on their farms hams and bacon for their own consumption, for their families and the hired workers who were provided with their board. Pigs were killed during the Winter, and frosty weather was preferred. "Whacker" was a noted slaughterer, and he provided a service for all the farmers within a reasonable distance of his cottage. He was a Chapel Sunday School teacher, and he was ever ready to give a lad who misbehaved a "whack," hence his nickname.

He provided the long scalding tub and the following tools: a punch, a heavy mallet, several knives and scrapers. Humane killers had not been invented, and in a slaughter-house pigs were knocked down with a felling axe — a round iron head from which a punch protruded was fixed to a shaft. It was a hit and miss affair, and the pigs suffered accordingly.

A pig was killed in the fold-yard on a patch of clean wheat straw. A plough-string was tied to its upper jaw, and when this was pulled taut the pig refused to move. While it was in this position "Whacker" held his punch fixed to a holder on the pig's forehead. Dick Dale, wagoner at The Grange, could drop a pig unconscious with one blow of the mallet. There was little doubt that the blood-letting was painless.

When life became extinct, the carcass was placed in the tub and boiling water was poured over it until it was covered. This treatment loosened the hairs on the carcass and scraping them off was no problem. When this work was completed the carcass was hung from a beam in the barn and then dressed. Several days later, when the flesh had become cold and firm, the carcass was removed to an outhouse where it was cut into four sections, each of which was covered with salt.

I never knew the exact details of the curing procedure, but there were no failures on the farms where I lived. The cured hams and sides were hung from the beams in the dairy, and they created an appetising picture. Today, hams and bacon produced on a farm would be condemned as unfit for human consumption. Perhaps the farming community was immune against food-poisoning, because this was unknown when I was employed as a hired worker.

Every weekday for breakfast and supper we were served with boiled fat bacon, dry bread and jam or fruit pies. A pie was passed round the table from one man to another, and each one cut a portion from left to right. The pie was cut in such a manner that a small piece the shape of a diamond was left in the middle to be eaten with the last portion. A "least lad" who failed to practise this procedure was liable to feel a rap on his fingers from the foreman's knife.

Similar meals were provided for hired workers who lived in on all the Wold farms, and the same method was practised when cutting a piece of pie. From 7.00 a.m. until noon work in the fields continued without a break unless one was necessary. A food helping of fat boiled bacon discouraged the pangs of hunger. Perhaps Bob Hadge had this in mind when he made the following remarks: "Ah hires six lads at Martimus an thar niva sick, tired, nor sorry. Ivary year Ah kills six pigs an thars nowt left bi tarm Martimus cums roond agee-an."

Bob worked beside his men and they all sat down at the same table to have their meals. Regardless of the good fare provided, their washing facilities before breakfast were primitive to the extreme. Fixed to the outside wall of the kitchen, near the door, was a lean-to shed open to all weathers. Underneath, placed on a table, was a piece of soap, a wash-basin, a towel, and a ladle-can. The latter was used to obtain rain-water which had run off the roof into a barrel. Usually after a hard frost the water was covered with ice.

These conditions brought the colour to men's faces, and a "least lad" was never troubled with pimples. He was the last to get washed, and when his turn came the towel was in a bonny state and he made do with a "lick and a promise." From his position at the table he was unable to see the fire, and he had to make up for time lost in order to satisfy his appetite. At 7.00 a.m. prompt Bob led his men out of the kitchen and the "least lad" was expected to follow.

In the Spring Bob continually worried until the corn was sown, and likewise during the Summer when fallows were being cultivated and sown with turnip seed. When wet weather held up harvest operations for several days, such was Bob's anxiety that he could neither eat nor sleep. He wore breeches and box-cloth leggings, and his legs became so thin that his breeches slipped downwards until his leggings folded over his boots to resemble concertinas. On one occasion the shepherd said: "If weather disant tack up see-an tawd man will slip clean throo is breeches."

On Lady Day, April 5th, 1929, Bob did not renew the lease of his farm, and in the March of the following year a sale of his live and dead stock took place. Tools, harnesses and implements were referred to as dead stock and were the first to be sold. There was a poor demand, and they were knocked down at rock bottom prices. Bob was so exasperated that he accused the auctioneer: "Thoos givin mi stuff away!"

When the threshing machine came under the hammer a bidder noticed that the tarpaulin sheet which should have covered it was to be sold as a separate lot. When he complained, Bob replied: "If thoo gans t tailor for a noo soot e disant gi that a top coat t gan wiv it!"

Farm sales were always held in March and they were advertised in local country papers. When a sale concerned a big farm there was an impressive list of horses, and particulars of each one were given. The following is a typical example: "Brown horse, Punch, 5 years old," or "Bay mare, 6 years old, in foal." A horse above the age of eight years was referred to as "aged." The numbers of three-year-olds, two-year-olds and yearlings were quoted, also information such as "broken to work in traces."

The horses were sold last in the afternoon, and if rain held up operations on the land, neighbouring farmers allowed their hired workers time off to see the horses sold. Men formed a selling ring, and each horse in turn was brought into the centre to be examined by prospective buyers.

The horses varied in size, age and quality, and bids were made accordingly. The five and six-year-old horses suitable for town work were bought by reputable dealers who suppied the railways or other firms. Local farmers bought the brood mares and young horses, but it was a sad day for those near the end of their working life. Bred and reared on the farm they had given good service and earned their keep. In Winter there had been sufficient fodder and an abundant supply of straw for bedding. The horses had been cared for by doting farm lads, and in the Summer they had grazed in grass fields. It was unlikely that they would experience similar conditions again.

The older horses were bought by unscrupulous dealers known as "long whippt uns." They drugged them in order to stimulate their actions and also doctored their legs to hide blemishes. Then they sent the horses to an auction mart where the flotsam and jetsam of the horse world were sold. The breeds varied from ponies to Shires, and none was guaranteed docile or sound.

The old farm horses being trotted in the ring was a pathetic sight to those who loved and understood horses. They were bought by hawkers or carting agents whose businesses were often hand-to-mouth affairs, and they kept their horses in back street stables. Unlike farmers who produced fodder, this had now to be bought. Consequently the horses were fed sparingly, and straw for bedding was in short supply. Their condition deteriorated: they lost flesh, and their rib cages began to show. Dilapidated harness caused the horses discomfort, for if a collar lacked stuffing, chains came into contact with a horse's body.

Some carting agents not satisfied with working their horses six days a week yoked them to wagonettes. On a Sunday they pulled these full of passengers out of a town into the country or to the seaside. Perhaps when the horses passed a grass field they would remember happier days spent grazing. When Bob sold up, sooner than let an old mare he had bred fall into dubious hands he had her put down.

34 HORSES

1. Bay Mare, Blossom, aged.
2. Bay Horse, Cobby, aged.
3. Bay Mare, Patch, aged.
4. Chestnut Mare, Smart, aged.
5. Bay Horse, Royal, aged.
6. Bay Horse, Bill, aged.
7. Bay Horse, Tom, aged.
8. Black Mare, Mettle, aged, in Foal.
9. Brown Horse, Tinker, aged.
10. Bay Mare, Doll, aged.
11. Brown Horse, Punch, 9 years old.
12. Black Mare, Darkie, 9 yrs., in Foal.
13. Bay Mare, Star, 6 yrs. old, in Foal.
14. Black Mare, Bonny, 5 years old.
15. Bay Horse, Boxer, 5 years old.
16. Bay Mare, Depper, 5 years old.
17. Bay Horse, Pilot, 5 years old.
18. Black Mare, Fan, 5 years, in Foal.
19. Brown Horse, Banker, 5 years old.
20. Brown Horse, Badger, 5 years old.
21. Brown Mare, Daisy, 4 years old.
    3 Three-year-olds.
    5 Two-year-olds.
    5 Yearlings.

130 BEASTS

23 Cows and Heifers, in Calf.
50 Store Bullocks, 2-2½ years old.
32 Store Bullocks, 1 year old.
25 Calves.

170 SHEEP

165 Ewes and Followers. 5 Rams.

30 PIGS

30 Sows, Pigged and in Pig.

IMPLEMENTS

9 Pole Wagons, 5 Heavy Carts, 3 Cambridge Rollers, 2 13-Spouted Corn Drills, Cultivator, 5 Binders, 2 Horse Rakes, 3 Horse Hoes, 3-Sheaf-Press, 2-Furrow Plough, 10 Wood Ploughs, 10 Diggers, Manure Drill, 8 Sets Gib Chisel Harrows, 2 Sail Reapers, 2 Sets Seed Harrows, Grass Reaper, Tip Reaper, 2 Swing Chisels, Scruffler, **Threshing Machine & Elevator, Fordson Tractor,** Mustard Drill, Water Cart, 2 Cart Jacks, 2 Knife Stands, Rully complete, 8 Stretchers, 12 Sets Plough Draughts, 8 3-Horse Baulks, 2 4-Horse Baulks, 2 Pig Feeders, 12 Pig Troughs, Grinding Mill, Grindstone, 2 Winnowing Machines, 2 Running Barrows, 2 Sets Weighs and Weights, Wheelbarrow, 2 Turnip Cutters, 2 Cake Crushers, 2 Lifting Barrows, Sack Bin, 2 Buggies, 2 Wagon Sheets, Quantity of Old Wood and Iron, Quantity Wire Nets and Bars, Etc.

Sale catalogue of live and dead stock, Saltaugh Grange Farm, Spring 1934.

75

CHAPTER TWENTY

During my employment at The Grange there were two occasions when, instead of bacon, we were served with ham. The harvest festival held in the local village chapel was well attended by the farming fraternity, and hired workers swelled the congregation too. They occupied the back seats and competed with the choir when hymns were sung.

Each year the service was conducted by a farm foreman who was a local preacher. His education had been limited, and when he was reading the Bible and was unable to pronounce a word he would hesitate then say: "An sike an sike a wod." The Chapel was decorated with flowers, and there was a good display of fruit and vegetables, as well as three sheaves — oats, barley and wheat — and the foreman's model corn stack.

The following night, after the produce had been sold, a supper was provided, home cooked by members. There was a good portion of ham, and a variety of cakes — a rare treat for hired workers. A concert followed, and ballads sung were appropriate for the occasion.

My grandfather often mentioned the "mell suppers" farmers in the past had provided for their workers after all had been gathered in. The custom had practically died out, and I was surprised when informed that a similar meal would be provided on this farm — an occasion I never experienced again.

Ham was included in the meal, which was as enjoyable as the one provided by the Chapel members, but the songs we sung, accompanied on a melodion played by Dick Dale, were not so refined. There was beer on tap, and droll tales were told in dialect, which contributed to the humour. It was midnight when we retired, and we were all merry. The next morning there were some heavy heads, but no complaints, and it was work as usual.

The last load of sheaves to arrive at the stackyard was always a welcome sight, whatever the harvest weather conditions had been. There was some loose corn left in the fields to gather, but there was less concern about this. Working until it was too dark to see came to an end. Autumn was on the wane: the harvest moon had passed and the countryside was beginning to look "backendish." Trees were shedding their leaves, and the hedgerows were turning brown.

Turnips were the only roots grown on the Wold farms. We were not subjected to the back-breaking work of lifting worzels or potatoes such as was experienced on low-lying farms. This was the reason we were able to plough for wheat as soon as the harvest was over. Four ploughs were at work, and a press drill followed the last one. The seed dropped between the ridges, and when they were harrowed level the seed was covered.

We ensured that each furrow was plumb straight, and the result was the straight rows of young wheat which could be seen throughout the Winter.

A full stackyard, with iron model of a fox protruding from each pike.

This method of sowing wheat as the land was ploughed was an operation I enjoyed.

A full stackyard was a fine sight and a reward for all the hard work which had been involved. On a moonlight night dark shadows were cast among the picturesque pikes, their "morpins" proudly pointing to the sky. Already one was missing: it had been threshed. Oats and chaff were required as fodder for the horses, straw for bedding and wheat to sow.

At this time of year grass was on the wane and poor fodder for the horses. Jim and myself continually haggled the foreman until he allowed us to sleep the horses in the stable. The first night must have been a welcome change for them. Instead of being turned out at the end of the day into the cold air to forage in a grass field, their bellies were full, and they had a good bed of straw to lie on. To see the horses so comfortable gave me a sense of satisfaction. I preferred stable work to walking in the early morning darkness, sometimes in the rain, to the pasture to collect the horses.

After wheat was sown, a start was made to plough the stubble fields. In between there were threshing days, and for Dick and myself there were journeys to Pocklington station with our wagons loaded with sold grain to be despatched by rail. Cattle had been brought into buildings to spend the Winter there. There was an increase in the amount of feeding-cakes required, and we transported these from the station to the farm.

In November the days were getting shorter, and once again we rode our plough horses to the field in darkness and likewise on our return journey home at the end of the day. Martinmas Day was drawing near, and the run up was a relaxed period. The horses benefitted too. Throughout harvest and wheat sowing there had been little respite for them.

We were looking forward to our pay day. We counted the days and eventually the hours. It was not difficult to pick the horsemen who would be asked to "stop again." The soft soaping they received was obvious. I was not surprised when Jim the foreman gave me this opportunity, but alas I had to turn it down. I was reluctant to leave this farm as I had been to leave Abbey Farm the previous year, but my uncle had asked me to return home to be his wagoner. I regretted leaving the two black horses I had worked and cared for throughout the year. It was natural to wonder whether they would be receiving similar treatment from the chap who followed me.

In future Martinmas Weeks when I met Jim at the Malton Hirings he offered to engage me to be the wagoner at The Grange, but I never returned. 1920 had been a difficult year for farmers, with prices obtained for stock and produce continually falling. At the hirings farmers offered reduced yearly wages which many wagoners would not accept, and they were unable to obtain places. Returning home relieved me of any anxiety in this respect.

At this time of the year the tidy appearance of Bill's farm compared favourably with that of a well-kept garden. The hedges had been trimmed with a slasher and the grass near the roots mown with a scythe. The grass and hedge clippings had been raked to form heaps before being carted into the middle of a field and burned. The stackyard had a tidy appearance too. There was no straw for burning and therefore no charred stubbles to blacken the landscape.

Bill's farm was a mixed one in the true sense of the word. Well maintained hedges were essential in the Summer to enclose pastures in order to prevent stock from straying. He was an expert hedger, and when gaps appeared they were plugged with stakes. A hedge in this state was allowed to grow freely for several years, and then it was eventually "cut and laid.'

This took place in the Winter when the sap was at its lowest ebb. The tools required were an axe, a saw and a bill-hook. Bill began work at one end of a hedge and continued in the same vein until it was completed. He removed the oldest branches and left the youngest and straightest. These were trimmed and then cut to the required length. A sliced cut was made with the bill-hook near the bottom of each one. This enabled Bill to lay each branch at a slight upward angle. It was important to make this cut as shallow as possible to enable each branch to maintain a good connection with its roots. Each branch overlapped part of the previous one laid, and to hold them in position small stakes were used. When completed the newly formed hedge was approximately two feet high.

In the Spring shoots appeared on the laid branches which would eventually become the foundation for a strong young hedge, but expert attention was required before it was brought to full fruition. The surplus thorns suitable for firewood were carted home to swell the stick hill situated at one end of the stackyard. When a ploughing match took place there was a competition for hedges. The skill hedgers had acquired has practically died out today.

CHAPTER TWENTY-ONE

It was four years since I had left home, and it was good to return and once again feel I was one of the family. During the Winter Bill was fully occupied looked after his stock. Ploughing, cultivating and sowing was my responsibility, and we rarely worked beside each other. It was different in the Summer when stock was turned out to grass and turnip hoeing or hay-time was in progress. On these occasions we worked until 9.00 p.m. when necessary.

In July Bill bought a BSA motorbike and sidecar — one of the first to appear in this area. One day when he was having a trial run he crashed the machine into the gate which opened into the lane. Fortunately it was an old one and the cross pieces broke. There was no visible damage to the bike, but it was assumed that the steerage had been affected.

The first time Bill rode his bike round the countryside his passenger was my grandfather. On their return he said: "The deng things over low. Ah cuddent see over edge tops, and if Ah add it went that fast Ah sud eu see-an nowt." This amused me because I could ride my pushbike as fast as Bill rode his machine.

On a Market Day he sailed through the gate into the lane with my Aunt Ella in the sidecar. There was no sign of the steerage being faulty, but this came to light in July when Bill and his friend Pa Thompson visited the Yorkshire Show. It was held in Hull, and they arrived without mishap, but on the return journey the steering locked. The machine swerved off the road onto the grass verge, mounted a bank, and turned over.

They were travelling at a slow speed and neither of them suffered any injury and they arrived home safely. Pa was wearing a new coat, and when he had explained to his wife the reason why they were late, she asked — much to Bill's amusement: "Ess thoo torn thy noo coat?"

Prior to 1919 there was no football played by farm workers, but on fine Summer evenings they could be seen playing cricket — a game they loved and understood. At the outbreak of war in 1914 the local team stored their gear in an outhouse at the rear of the Black Bull, about a mile from Pickering. When peace was declared the team was re-formed, but a few of the old faces were missing. Their owners lay in the fields of Flanders, and their places were taken by players such as myself who had been too young to go to war.

Our recognised cricket field was Bob Berryman's horse pasture, and we prepared a wicket in the middle where the grass was short. We borrowed his horse-drawn water cart and brought water from a pond to soften the surface, then we pushed Bob's flat roller over it to level the bumps. On a Saturday afternoon we biked miles to away matches and carried our gear.

During the Summer there was occasional rain and the land was never short of moisture. This created good pasturage and corn crops were excellent too. The ears were well filled, turnips were also doing well and heavy crops were expected. Harvest was early and cutting began the first week in August. We made such good progress that Bill allowed me to attend the Scarborough Cricket Festival.

This began the first week in September. Yorkshire v MCC was the first match, followed by a gentlemen versus players match. On the last three days Mr Levison Gower's XI played the current touring side. The eleven were picked from test players, and the match had the status of a test match. Their opponents were an Australian team, the first to tour this country after the 1914-18 war. They never lost a match until they played Mr Levinson Gower's XI.

It was the last match of the tour, and I was privileged to see the last day's play. I cannot remember the details, but I can recall the names of several players who took part. Warrick Armstrong, the captain, had played in test matches in England as far back as 1902. In his team were Collins, Bardsley, McCartney and Mailey, one of the world's best googly bowlers. During the Summer his two fast bowlers, Gregory and McDonald, had been the scourge of England's batsmen. Few had escaped damaged fingers when facing Gregory.

It was impossible to forget such names as Hobbs, Rhodes, Whooley, Tydesly, Hearne, or Patsy Hendren, who were members of the England team. Spectators had a great respect for them and they looked upon the wicket as if it were hallowed ground.

1921 was for me a memorable year. I saw an Australian test team play and I travelled in a motor bus for the first time. It was one of two owned by Abraham and Stephens, Pickering men who provided a service to and from Scarborough.

The following year was marred by the death of my grandfather, who had had such an influence over me in my boyhood days. We also lost our old dog Punch and another link with those days was broken. After the wheat had been sown at backend, Bill informed me that he was going to retire in the following Spring and sell up. I decided to attend Pickering Hirings and obtain another place.

During the afternoon I met a friend who told me that J. B. Armitage of Hagg House Farm was seeking a wagoner. Eventually we found him, and after inquiries regarding my background he engaged me for the yearly wage of £45. Hagg House is situated between Pickering and Thornton-le-Dale and stands on an incline about half a mile from the road. It could be seen clearly from our stackyard, and I little dreamt that I should live and work on this farm.

The following June I was informed that my pair of horses and wagon would be required to convey Sunday School scholars on their annual outing. I had already begun preparations — cleaning harnesses etc. — when news came through that other arrangements were being made — much to my disappointment.

Pickering Sunday School Outing, 1922. Wagon belonged to J. B. Armitage of Hagg House Farm. W. Stead is wagoner in picture.

CHAPTER TWENTY-TWO

1922 was the last year Pickering Sunday School scholars travelled in farm wagons on their annual Summer outing. The wagons had been washed or repainted for the occasion. The horses were well groomed and their manes plaited with gaily coloured ribbons. Harness and horse brasses had been polished and bright hames were attached to the horses' collars. The whole assembly glittered in the afternoon sunshine of a July day.

At a pre-arranged time after their mid-day meal, children and their teachers met in the Market Place where the wagons stood in line. Children were dressed in their Sunday best clothes, and each one carried a mug and a plate. A tea urn and the food required were conveyed in a wagon. Soon the procession was on its way to Park Gates or further afield where suitable fields had been loaned.

The clip-clop of horses' shoes and the knapping caused by the wagon wheels mingled with the laughter of happy children. The procession created a scene which will never be witnessed again.

On arrival at the destination the wagons were soon empty of passengers. Sports were organised for the oldest children, while the rest played games. Each scholar received a bag of sweets and later a tea was served. In the evening they returned in the wagons to the Market Place where parents were waiting to welcome them. Quite a crowd had gathered. Many not concerned with the children had come to admire the horses and wagons.

In the following year, 1923, a committee was formed from the members of the various denominations. They decided to charter a train to give the children and those who wished to accompany them a joint Sunday School outing to Scarborough. No praise could be too high for those who organised these trips. Throughout the years they took place there was never a serious mishap. The names of those who intended going were recorded several weeks in advance of the arranged date. A week before, railway tickets were collected from the respective Sunday Schools. Food was provided by parents and friends: it was packed in boxes which were conveyed to Scarborough in an earlier train accompanied by the teachers. Arrangements had previously been made between the Pickering denominations and similar ones in Scarborough for the use of the latters' school rooms. These were recognised as the headquarters where teachers prepared meals, and one was served to the trippers on their arrival.

The outing took place on the first Wednesday in July, which was a half day closing for the shops. The train was due to leave at 10.00 a.m., but long before that the parents and children began to congregate in Park Street near the station. Each religious sect formed a group and travelled in the carriages reserved for them. Due to the length of the train it had to be moved forward in stages. When it departed the engine coughed and

Sunday School trippers congregated in Park Street, Pickering, waiting their turn to board the train.

belched black smoke until the wheels turned freely. A ghost town was left behind. No Pied Piper could have taken the children away so quickly or completely as the long train.

On arrival at Scarborough the children were taken to their allotted destination to enjoy the meal prepared. The rest of the day was their own to spend with their parents, but they were expected to return by 4.30 p.m. This enabled the children to be washed and cuts and bruises treated before tea was served. The day's outing was drawing to a close. The train was due to leave Scarborough at 6.30 p.m. The youngest passengers knew little about the return journey — tired out they soon fell asleep. Every year the number of trippers increased until there were more than one train could accommodate and two were chartered.

This event took place in an economic depression when children's lives were very drab. Due to low wages and unemployment, poverty was rife, yet parents and friends contributed in every possible manner to make the outing a happy day for the children, and they succeeded.

In July 1972 the following appeared in a local paper: "A tradition which for one day brought shops and offices in Pickering to a standstill is to vanish. For the first time for over half a century there will be no joint Sunday School outing. The decision was reached at a recent meeting of the committee representing the four Sunday Schools at Pickering."

"Horse-drawn vehicles were the first to set up the pilgrimage when they conveyed their excited passengers to neighbouring fields where sports were arranged and tea supplied. Between the two World Wars when the age of steam was supreme and Sunday Schools had large populations it was not unusual for over a thousand children and parents in two excursion trains to make the trip to Scarborough. Large crowds met in Park Street to herald the departure and arrival of the trains. With the disappearance of the railway and the emergence of the family motor car the number has rapidly declined. Last year only 170 went by coach and even fewer seem likely to respond this year, so the committee decided it was impractical to continue the outing on the same basis. The only course was to leave each individual Sunday School to arrange its outing if it wished to do so."

CHAPTER TWENTY-THREE

During the depression experienced in the 1920s, farming was at its lowest ebb. Never in living memory had the price of cereals been so low: for example, wheat was sold for £1 a quarter. An Agricultural Wages Board had been formed which fixed rates of pay according to age. Bargaining at the hirings no longer took place, but the custom of a worker receiving a fest after he had agreed to be hired continued.

The yearly wage fixed for a wagoner aged twenty-one or over was £43.70. Before the 1914-18 War wheat had made thirty-five shillings a quarter, and the highest yearly wage a wagoner received was £20. In those days farming was certainly a more profitable business.

The farmers hardest hit by the depression were the tenants of big farms where a large labour force was required. When one became vacant there was a poor demand for the tenancy. A landlord was willing to let a big farm for as low as 2s. 6d. an acre in order to keep the land under cultivation. Each year in March a large number of farm sales were held and some were the result of bankruptcy.

No member of the farming community worked harder than a foreman's wife who provided board for the hired men. At Abbey Farm four of us lived in and Mrs Bean also brought up four daughters and a son. She had little time for leisure, and she rarely left the house except to attend an evening service in the village church. It was due partly to her industry and care that her husband eventually became a farmer.

During the war, Bob, her husband, had earned good money, and between them they had saved sufficient to stock a small farm. The first few years were a hard struggle mainly because Bob had to work hard. When their family had grown up, life for both of them became easier.

In order to economise, farmers reduced the labour force they required in the Winter, and this caused unemployment. In the Summer, the busiest time of the year, there was work to be had but this came to an end after the harvest had been gathered and roots lifted. During the Winter the only work available for the out-of-work farm worker was the odd day's threshing, and there was poverty in the villages.

Prior to 1920 a wagoner who was a good hand with horses could obtain the maximum yearly wage, but this no longer applied when wages were fixed. Extra hours worked in the stable were classified as paid overtime for the first time. Before this came into force farmers used to complain if they thought insufficient time was spent in the stable. Now the majority of them reduced the time spent at each session to one hour in order to cut costs. Consequently there was some neglect, and in some cases the interest in horses began to wane, but this did not apply to my horses. The number of hours — paid or unpaid — that I spent in the stable I considered to be my business only. Old habits died hard.

At the hirings farmers were inclined to ignore wagoners twenty-one and over. They engaged younger workers whose rates of pay were lower. Many had no experience of life on a farm when horses had been essential animals. When a tractor was available there was no lack of volunteers to drive it. Riding over clots was certainly more comfortable than walking on them.

One-man bus companies had been formed and they operated between villages and towns. There were no official bus stops, and it was not unusual to hear a passenger remark to the driver: "Stop at next loo-an Fred an pick ooa Lizz." When I was the wagoner at Mount Pleasant Farm, Sawdon, I used to travel by bus to Scarborough on a Saturday afternoon, especially in the Summer. After tea I attended a cinema at the boys' price of 1/-.

Clothes could be bought off the peg. I bought my suits from Burtons, where they had my exact size in stock .Village tailors could not compete with their prices, and the writing on the wall for them was evident. It was a far cry from the days when corduroy bell-bottoms were the vogue and work continued throughout Saturdays.

The hiring system was continued into the 1930s, and perhaps today this manner of employment may be considered to be degrading. This did not occur to me, as I had a good life on the farms where I lived and worked. I enjoyed the best of health, and the cost of my clothes was my only essential expense. In the towns and cities there was poverty unparallelled today, and there were unemployed industrial workers who, given the chance, would have accepted a guaranteed year's work and their board regardless of the reward. Some did visit the farms, but they had no chance of obtaining work when there was a surplus of experienced workers.

Farmers who could afford to do so were turning to tractors which ran on paraffin, but petrol was required to start them. Men soon learned to drive the tractors: after all, it was a simple matter when compared to handling a pair of frisky horses. However, a certain amount of ingenuity had to be practised when coupling a tractor to a horse-drawn implement. In the early stages the only one designed for tractor power was a double furrow plough. A man rode on it and jacked it up at the headland mark by means of a lever. Farmers considered that the man was wasting his time, and in the future a plough was designed which enabled the tractor driver to operate it.

Due to the position of the new exhaust pipe, these early machines were a health hazard. It was not unusual to see a driver's clothes covered with a film of grease and dust which no doubt affected his health. I never operated a tractor if I could avoid it: I preferred following horses.

Armitage of Hagg House, Pickering, was one of the first farmers in the area to own a tractor. When I was the wagoner I ensured that when cultivating fallows the machine was coupled to the implements that did the donkey work such as a drag or heavy roller. I am sure no-one realised at the time that the use of tractors was the first step to complete mechanisation. Certainly no-one would have believed that some day farms would be without horses.

Fordson tractor at work ploughing on Hagg House Farm, Pickering, in 1923.

NATIONAL UNION OF AGRICULTURAL WORKERS

Head Office: Headland House, 308 Gray's Inn Road, London W.C.   General Secretary, R. B. Walker

East Riding of Yorkshire Wages 1926-27

Male Workers living in net wages 51 weeks to the year

	Per week	Per year
Foremen not hinds	17s. 0d.	£43 7s. 0d.
Waggoners	13s. 0d.	£33 3s. 0d.
Third lads (carry corn)	12s. 0d.	£30 12s. 0d.
Third lads (not carry)	10s. 0d.	£25 10s. 0d.
Fourth lads	9s. 0d.	£22 19s. 0d.
Waggoner lads	7s. 0d.	£17 17s. 0d.
Other horse lads	6s. 0d.	£13 15s. 0d.
Least lads	5s. 6d.	£12 10s. 0d.
Beastmen and Shepherds	14s. 0d.	£35 15s. 0d.

Male Workers not living in

Age 21 years and over	35/-
Age 20 to 21	32/-
Age 19 to 20	30/-
Age 18 to 19	29/-
Age 17 to 18	26/-
Age 16 to 17	23/-
Age 15 to 16	18/-
Age 14 to 15	15/-

Hours of Work

48 hours per week in Winter and 52½ hours in Summer with not more than 12 hours per week-days for stable work and attention to stock 3 hours allowed on Sundays.

Rent: Cottage with 3 bedrooms 3/- per week

Rent: Cottage with 2 bedrooms 2/- per week

Potatoes 6d. per stone

Milk wholesale price

Such a notice would be published in every country paper concerned with farming.

CHAPTER TWENTY-FOUR

In 1925 the produce sold off the land in Great Britain totalled £300,000,000 for the year, with a limited number of farmers starting to use tractors. The cost of a tractor was £350, and no doubt their numbers would have been larger if farmers had been more prosperous.

The first demonstration of a combine harvester and artificial grain drier took place on a Wiltshire farm in 1928. A combine with a cutting width of six feet cost £260, and larger machines were between £400 and £450. It was estimated that the cost of mechanising a farm was about £5 to £6 an acre. Labour was nine pence an hour, petrol 1s. 3d. per gallon, and paraffin 7½d. a gallon. The following is a summary of the cost per acre of horse-drawn operations as opposed to tractor power.

	Horses	Tractor
Ploughing per acre	12s. 6d. to 20s. 0d.	4s. 6d. to 7s. 6d.
Cultivation per acre	2s. 6d. to 49s. 0d.	2s. 3d. to 2s. 9d.
Rolling per acre	1s. 6d. to 2s. 0d.	1s. 0d. to 1s. 3d.
Harrowing per acre	1s. 6d. to 2s. 9d.	1s. 0d. to 1s. 6d.
Drilling per acre	3s. 6d. to 5s. 6d.	1s. 2d. to 1s. 6d.
Harvesting per acre	30s. 0d. to 40s. 0d.	15s. 0d. to 20s. 0d.

For harvesting the comparison was made between cutting, stooking, leading, stacking and threshing and a combine harvester plus a grain drier. During the 1930s a combine was in use on a Sherburn Wold farm, but the owner went out of business before war broke out in 1939. At the time nobody believed that harvesting with a combine would be a success. Farming conditions were quite different from those experienced in America, where there were wide-open prairies and combines had been in operation for many years.

Cost comparisons between horses and machines are often made today in favour of horses, but only farmers who have experienced both types of farming are capable of making a correct assessment. They know the advantages to be obtained from using machines and the time saved. Time is money, especially when the weather plays such an important part in farming operations. The initial outlay may be larger, but less labour is required, which is an important economic factor. Instead of growing oats for horse fodder a more profitable crop can be produced. With a combine, the harvest is gathered in a matter of days instead of weeks.

Nor is there the expense which was incurred on a threshing day. Farm workers were well rid of that detestable operation. At the end of the day a combine can be sheeted down and forgotten until the next day. No early morning rising to prepare horses or evening work in the stable. There are no blacksmith's or saddler's bills to meet. Nor is it necessary for farmers' wives to board workers or help with the harvest.

Among the most pleasant aspects of the countryside are the crops of ripening corn, but they no longer create such picturesque scenes as those witnessed in the past. The ears are not the same rich golden colour and the stalks are shorter. The width of the drill rows has been reduced from eight inches to four. More ground is covered with seed and by this means higher yields are produced, but the movements of the stalks are restricted. This is the reason that you rarely see them swaying to and fro in a strtong breeze or hear the swish created by barley horns when the ears brush together.

The photograph on the following page of a pleasant harvest scene was obtained in the late 1950's, a short time before combines appeared on the scene. Regardless of the number of tractors used on the land during the 1930's, horses held their own. During the next two decades there was an improvement in the design of tractors and implements. Their numbers increased too, and horses were gradually phased out.

Those featured in this photograph were the last pair to be retained by John Stavely, a Wold farmer. It is evident that they were in peak condition and most likely in semi-retirement. I imagine they were grazing in a pasture when the corn was being cut in the next field and were able to watch a tractor towing a binder. The horses would not be yoked to the machine again, yet when the time came to lead the sheaves home they played an important part.

A tractor was at a disadvantage when the trailer coupled to it was being loaded in a field, because an extra man was required to drive it from one stack to another. A forker could direct a pair of horses yoked to a wagon by word of mouth. Only two words were required, "Gee up" and "Woa." To solve this problem the horses pulled the trailer until it was loaded.

A shuttle service was operated, with the tractor towing the loaded trailer to the stackyard and an empty one then returning to the field where a third tractor was being loaded. The changeover of a trailer from horses to the tractor was completed in the minimum of time. This would have been impossible if the horses had been yoked direct to the trailer. A horse-drawn vehicle could not have been directed unless the horses had been yoked — one at each side of a pole which was connected to the horses' hames.

This ingenious "yoked up" was the complete answer to the problem. It could be described as unique, because nothing of the kind had been practised in the past. The draw-bar attached to a trailer was removed and replaced with the fore-carriage of a farm wagon — two wheels, a pole, and two swingletrees. When the horses moved on between stooks they were able to control the movements of the trailer. Also, when the exchange of two trailers took place, the fore-carriage could be coupled or uncoupled in the same manner as when the tractor was involved.

93

Loading a trailer with sheaves of corn on a Wolds Farm

There is no doubt that this procedure as a whole cut costs and reduced the time required to gather the sheaves. A trailer was longer and wider than a wagon, and therefore bigger loads were carried which reduced the number of journeys to and from a field. The two fine horses were enjoying the good life, but their days were numbered. The farm was on the verge of being completely mechanised.

The following harvest a combine appeared on the scene, and corn was cut and threshed in one operation. Sheaves are no longer produced, and the special skill involved when loading or stacking the sheaves has become obsolete too.

CHAPTER TWENTY-FIVE

Bill Baxter owned Manor Farm, which was considered to be a good place for hired workers and for horses too, until his son, Bob, returned from College. Ideas he had learned there and which he attempted to put into practice caused a lot of trouble. His first project concerned costing and recording the amounts of oats the horses ate each day, but this was soon knocked on the head. When Bob suggested that the horses' rations should be reduced, the feeders not only protested, but also threatened to leave *en bloc*.

His second project, timing men at work, was a failure too. Muck leading was in progress, four wagons being in use, and because each load carried was identical, the timing was perfect. There were two men "standing fillers" in the fold yard, and it so happened that Thoddy's wagon was being loaded. Farm workers as a whole were never afraid to make a stand for what they believed to be right. They certainly would not tolerate a man standing over them when they were at work. After the following incident, Bill ordered his son not to interfere with the general routine of the farm again.

When Bob appeared, pencil and paper in hand, and Thoddy saw him standing near the gate, he enquiried: "Wutts that youth effta?" "E's cum t tarm tha" was the reply. Thoddy had a certain reputation, and his reaction was expected. He stuck his fork into the manure with such force that the tines were buried, and then he walked to the gate and said to Bob: "If thoo isant oot o mi seet i two seconds ahl throw tha eead fost in tiv oss trough."

Bob disappeared, but within minutes he and his father returned. There could only be one result from the confrontation which followed. Thoddy left his fork stuck in the manure and his horses yoked to the wagon, collected the money he had earned to date and his box of belongings and left.

There was more trouble when Jim bought a tractor with iron cleats fixed to the iron wheels. It is not difficult to imagine the effect these had on the land when it was tender. Bob installed himself as the tractor driver, and there were occasions when the foreman would not allow the machine on the land, which caused more disagreements. Although Bob used to get people's backs up, no-one wanted the tragic end to the problem which eventually came about.

He had a craze for shooting, and no wild creature was safe if it came within range of his gun. One day, to my disgust, I saw him shoot an owl, and words passed between us. It was not unusual to hear a shot fired from his bedroom in the early hours of the morning. Bob carried his gun on the tractor and shot hares when they appeared in the field. This was not difficult, for only when the engine was stopped did they show signs of fear — remarkable, but quite true.

Austin tractor towing a binder, 1929.

One particular morning, when Bob was at work, he carried his cocked gun on the tractor. It accidentally triggered off, and as Bob slumped over the steering wheel, the tractor turned in the nearside lock. The accident was not discovered until the tractor was seen turning in circles.

It happened in June, and there was one field still to be cultivated and sown with turnip seed. Jack, the undershepherd, agreed to drive the tractor. At harvest it was coupled to a binder and to a plough when a start was made to sow wheat. When this operation was completed the tractor was stored in a shed throughout the winter. Jack returned to the sheepfold until the spring, when he was called upon to operate the tractor again.

With the aid of this machine the time which had been required in previous years to complete corn sowing was substantially reduced. Cultivation of the fallows followed, and again the tractor made its mark, with turnip seed being sown in record time. When Martinmas Day arrived changes took place, and life on this farm was never quite the same again.

The foreman was not retained, nor the two stable lads and a labourer. The wagoner agreed to include in his duties the responsibilities of a foreman, and he was hired for another year. Four of the twelve horses were sold, and the remaining eight were divided equally between the wagoner and a Thoddy. Although the depleted work-force, with the aid of a tractor, could manage cultivation and sowing, it was impossible for them to cope with the summer work such as hoeing turnips. The only answer to this problem was to engage casual workers, and they were plentiful. Nevertheless there were occasions when things did not run smoothly.

On all farms delivering sold grain to a railway station was recognised as the wagoner's and thoddy's responsibility. It was a welcome change from plodding after horses on the land, and provided a chance to show the horses off. All the horses in a goods yard were inspected by the wagoners concerned. When the wagoner learned that the grain was to be transported by tractor and trailer there was an unholy row. Thoddy joined in, and they both asked for their money to date in order to leave, but this was refused. The majority of wagoners who had experienced work in the pre-tractor era were not prepared to accept certain changes which took place on a farm where a tractor was available. At the first opportunity they found other employment.

The year was 1929 and it was to be my last as a farm wagoner. I was employed by Bill Pennock, who was the tenant of Mount Pleasant Farm, adjacent to Manor Farm. The changes and antics which had taken place on the latter were common knowledge. Bill was noted for his love of horses, and he had no desire to obtain a tractor.

Motor businesses were springing up — one-man affairs, with owner drivers — and they were keen to expand. Some converted their vehicles to enable them to transport farm stock to markets, and the old-time drovers went out of business. Agricultural merchants realised the advantages when farm produce was conveyed direct to its destination, and then products required by farmers could be brought straight from factories to farms.

During the 1930's motor haulage businesses became firmly established. The number of farm wagons travelling on the roads gradually decreased and eventually became obsolete. The days of the farm wagoners were numbered too, and some turned their hands to driving motor transport vehicles.

CHAPTER TWENTY-SIX

During the 1930's there was a noticeable increase in the number of farm tractors and implements designed for tractor towing. Traditional farming practices were continually changing. The old-time pre-1914 foreman had retired or passed on. The picturesque stacks they used to build were missing from many stackyards. Instead of thatch they were covered with a load of straw held in position with nets. The appropriate description for one of these was a "heap."

In 1936 the hiring system came to an end, and there were no places for the traditional wagoners. Single workers no longer lived in the respective farmhouses, and the horses were not kept to the same standard as in the past. But the changes which took place after the advent of the combine harvester were more drastic than anyone could have foreseen.

Horsemen were surprised and shocked at the speed with which the horses were slaughtered and replaced with machines. It was soon realised by the speed with which operations were completed that mechanisation was here to stay. Today cereals are sown at backend, and on a farm where no root crops are produced work on the land, except for spraying, is completed then until harvest time. It is possible for a businessman to own a farm, contract out the work involved in producing cereals, and at harvest sell the standing crops at a price per acre. This would have been impossible in the pre-tractor era when there was work of some description to do all the year around.

The passing of the horses was the start of the deterioration of the countryside. It is the small, mixed farms I miss the most. The horses, cattle and sheep, each breed grazing in a separate pasture sandwiched between crops, contributed to the country scene. Today there are no farms which function as such. The land has been sold to larger concerns, and the buildings not suitable for modern requirements have been left to deteriorate or have been bulldozed off the face of the earth.

> Shades of Rise Carr Farm
> Where I spent a happy boyhood.